Alan Palmer was educated at Bancroft's School, Essex, and Oriel College, Oxford. He was head of the History Department, Highgate School from 1953 to 1969. His many publications include *Alexander I, Metternich, Russia in War and Peace, The Gardeners of Salonika, Napoleon in Russia, Frederick the Great* and *The Penguin Dictionary of Modern History*. He has recently completed a biography of Bismarck to be published early in 1976.

THE LIFE AND TIMES OF GEORGE IV

Alan Palmer

Introduction by Antonia Fraser

CARDINAL edition published in 1975
by Sphere Books Ltd
30/32 Gray's Inn Road, London WC1X 8JL

First published in Great Britain by
Weidenfeld & Nicolson and Book Club Associates 1972
Copyright © George Weidenfeld & Nicolson and
Book Club Associates 1972

Set in Linotype Lectura

Printed in Great Britain by
Hazell Watson & Viney Ltd
Aylesbury, Bucks

CONTENTS

ACKNOWLEDGMENTS

Photographs and illustrations were supplied by or are reproduced by kind permission of the following. By gracious permission of HM the Queen, plates I, IV, 1, 2, 3, 4, 13, 14, 15, 36, 37, 38, 39, 40, 50, 53, 58, 60, 61; City of Birmingham Museums and Art Gallery, plate 27; Brighton Pavilion, plates VI, VII, 10, 11, 21, 45, 46; British Museum, plates III, V, VIII, IX, XI, 23, 30, 41, 48, 51, 54, 55, 56, 59; London Museum, plates 7, 43; Longmans Archives, plates 22, 44; Mansell Collection, plates 17, 18, 31, 47; National Gallery, plate 52; National Monuments Record, plate 42; National Portrait Gallery, plates 16, 24, 25, 26, 28, 29, 33, 49, 57; Radio Times Hulton Picture Library, plates 12, 19, 32; Royal Academy, plates 34, 35; Royal Institute of British Architects, plates 8, 9; Victoria and Albert Museum, plates 6, 20; Wallace Collection, plate 5; M. H. de Young Memorial Museum, San Francisco, plate II.

Extracts from George's letters are taken from *Correspondence of George as Prince of Wales*, edited by A. Aspinall, and are reproduced by permission of Cassell & Co. Ltd, and Oxford University Press, New York.

INTRODUCTION

There is certainly an interesting clash between the two widely-held public views of King George IV. On the one hand there is the notion of a young and gifted Prince, the golden-haired 'Florizel' of his youthful affair with the exquisite actress 'Perdita' Robinson. This is the Prince who, as ruler in place of his periodically deranged father, grew up to give his name to the devil-may-care age of the Regency, marked by a sartorial elegance personified by the Prince's friend, the supreme dandy Beau Brummell. The Prince's love affairs, numerous as they were, included a clandestine marriage – undertaken in order to seduce the affections of the otherwise impregnably virtuous Mrs Fitzherbert. All this is the very stuff of romantic novels, then and now.

The other side of the picture is so much less attractive as to be frankly rather ludicrous: the ageing self-indulgent 'Prinny' whom Brummell cruelly categorised as Alvanley's 'fat friend'; the sordid complications of his finances as heir to the throne; and the fact that the later mistresses were, almost to a woman, grandmothers. Then the Prince's official marriage to Princess Caroline of Brunswick began as a farce with a drunken wedding-night and ended in mockery – ironically it was the Princess rather than her husband who was tried in the English courts for adultery. Fate almost robbed the Prince of the reign which was his due: when his father, the old mad George III, finally died in 1820, there were only ten years left for George IV to enjoy as undisputed sovereign. Furthermore these were years bedevilled by the acute and complicated rivalries which marked post-Waterloo Britain, the age of Canning and Castlereagh, and finally of Wellington.

Yet somehow we feel that everything was conducted in an atmosphere of great taste and elegance, whether at Regency Brighton in the newly-constructed Oriental Pavilion, or among the classically-arcaded buildings with which John Nash was also glorifying London in the course

9

of his long and sympathetic partnership with the Prince Regent. It was characteristic of the style of the age that it produced Lord Byron and Jane Austen, both of whose works were greatly enjoyed by the Prince (the novel *Emma* was even, surprisingly enough, dedicated to him).

The enigma of the character of George IV was, as Alan Palmer shows, something which even his contemporaries felt at the time. Our own sense of a dichotomy merely echoes something innately paradoxical at the heart of his nature. Perhaps the truth lay in the extraordinary influences inherent in his upbringing, heir to the throne yet trained for nothing, destined for monarchy yet the natural focus for political opposition so long as his father reigned. It is indeed by placing George IV firmly against the background of his own time that Alan Palmer succeeds in freshly illuminating the character of this fascinating if baffling monarch. And at the same time he enriches our own concept of the ever-alluring, ever-dashing Regency period.

Antonia Fraser

I

Florizel 1762–85

The birth of the future George ɪv, like much of his later life, marred high expectations with a confusion which bordered on bathos. Everyone at the English Court had passed the hot summer days of 1762 awaiting news from the palace with lively interest. No heir had been born to a reigning monarch for nearly three-quarters of a century, not since the miraculously timed arrival of James ɪɪ's son, that 'Old Pretender' who was still living out his pious exile in Rome. Then, in 1688, absence of credible eye-witnesses had fed Whig ears with tales of warming pans and other nonsense: now the event was to be almost a public spectacle and St James's Palace, already cramped and crowded, teemed with dignitaries as soon as it was known, on the afternoon of 12 August, that Charlotte of Mecklenburg-Strelitz was in labour. The Archbishop of Canterbury, the First Lord of the Treasury, the two Secretaries of State, the officers of the Privy Council and of the Royal Household, all mingled a little incongruously with the Ladies of the Bedchamber and with Charlotte's German women attendants in the Queen's ante-room on that Thursday. George ɪɪɪ himself – in those days handsome, auburn-haired and only twenty-four – remained within the comparative privacy of his own apartments. But, as an affectionate husband and a conscientious sovereign, he was by no means indifferent to what was happening in the other set of rooms and he let it be known that he would give £500 to the bearer of news of a daughter, with the sum doubled if he learnt he had a son.

The child was born at twenty-four minutes past seven in the evening, as the Countess of Northumberland meticulously noted in her journal. At once the Earl of Huntingdon hurried to the King's rooms and informed George he was the father of a baby girl. It is not clear why Huntingdon, who was Master of the King's Horse, should have undertaken a mission which might have been effected with happier veracity if less despatch by the Lord Chamberlain, nor do we know what recompense, if any, was made to the Earl. But the King was grateful for the message. Having assured Huntingdon that he cared little about the sex of the child so long as the Queen's health was not in jeopardy, he went at once to Charlotte. Then he discovered she had given birth to 'a strong, large, pretty boy'. Lest any doubt remain, the new Prince was brought out and shown to the peers temporal and spiritual. He greeted his father's subjects lustily.

Five days after this precocious levée the royal infant was created Prince of Wales, and a week later members of the nobility were admitted, for two hours on six successive afternoons, to gaze on the heir of England, Scotland, Ireland and Hanover as he slept in a cot behind a lattice-work partition. The commonalty, less privileged, caught sight of him 'taking the air' in Hyde Park and cheered him as 'a jolly young dog'. It is sad to record that, in later years, he was never so popular with the Londoners as during those first weeks of innocence. On 16 September he was baptised George Augustus Frederick in a characteristically domestic ceremony. The christening took place, not in the chapel of St James's Palace where Laud had once sprinkled Jordan holy water over the future Charles II, but in the Queen's drawing-room; and there the total absence of all religious furnishings ensured that Archbishop Ecker would not be tempted to stray from the narrowly Germanic Protestantism upon which the King and his consort dutifully shaped their lives. George III, who was deeply moved by the simple baptismal liturgy, genuinely hoped that the young Prince, too, would learn to accept the moral respectability of his own faith. The King's father, grandfather and brothers and sisters were notoriously profligate; and the child's godfather, his great-uncle 'Butcher' Cumberland, showed a persistent insensibility to the nobler virtues; but George and Charlotte were determined that their sons and daughters – and there were fifteen of them in all – should be reared in a rigid code of restraint and austerity, relentlessly schooled for good living. Though the intention was admirable, it was psychologically disastrous.

Most of the Prince's childhood was spent in the rural isolation of the Bower Lodge at Kew or the privacy of Buckingham House, a comfortable red-brick building and not as yet a palace, which the King had purchased in the year of his son's birth. The boy was on show at the Queen's genteel Thursday 'drawing rooms' from an early age and, after his fifth birthday, he would be taken occasionally to the opera. Sometimes he made a formal appearance at State occasions, for he had been created Knight of the Garter at the age of three and a half. We hear of him a few months afterwards inoculated against smallpox (an idea of his mother) and a year later receiving a gift of twenty-one brass cannon, mounted on travelling carriages and firing balls of 1-lb calibre (an idea of his father). Yet, for the most part, his boyhood remains strangely artificial, as empty of character as the limpid family portraits commissioned from John Zoffany and Thomas Gainsborough. Lady Sarah Lennox, with whom George III had once been in love, wrote scathingly when the Prince was five years old that the King 'has made his brat the proudest little imp you ever saw', a judgment substantiated by every painting that survives; but the reminiscences of members of the Household suggest he already possessed a sense of humour and a devastating gift of mimicry which, as he had little to do but listen and observe the follies around him, was soon sharpened to perfection. The saddest feature of his early life was the absence of young companions outside the family, an omission which may have inclined him to cast interested eyes at the maids-of-honour attached to his sisters. His closest friend was his brother Frederick, Duke of York, a year his junior. Together the boys were encouraged to cultivate a strip of land at Kew, although neither shared the agricultural enthusiasm of their father. Despite the slight disparity of age, they attended the same classes for eight hours each day and, in time, learnt to ride and fence together. Often, too, they were flogged together, for the King fully shared the belief of his British and German compatriots in the educational virtues of the rod and the birch. The two boys remained inseparable until the close of 1780, when Frederick was sent to Hanover to complete that military education which would shortly win for him – and for 'ten thousand men' – a derisive immortality in English folk legend.

The Prince acquired a good knowledge of the Latin Classics, competence at French, German and Italian and some skill in music. His spelling, especially of English place names, was poor although less individualistic than his father's. He enjoyed Shakespeare but seems to have had little acquaintance with the other great works of English literature and, as George III once complained, had 'no insight into the springs . . . of Ancient and Modern History'. Though his father gave him little credit for his studies, he was intelligent and far more accomplished than most of the princelings in Europe. From the Earl of Holderness, who was in general charge of the education of both royal princes from 1771 to 1776, he gained good advice which was often sensibly delivered. There is even, in the Prince's printed correspondence, a gently ironic plea from Holderness that George should moderate his diet, written when the Prince was still some months short of his thirteenth birthday. Unfortunately he seems regularly to have forgotten his moral tutor's precepts as soon as they were delivered.

This waywardness is not entirely surprising. One Polonius, however sententious, might have succeeded in influencing the poor lad's character: three, and at times more, were insufferable. For ten years exhortations followed one another at irregular intervals from his parents and his tutors. On his eighth birthday he received the gift of a pocket book from his mother together with a letter in which the Queen – who, it should be remembered, was still a young woman of twenty-six – thundered moral rectitude with an almost Pauline intensity:

> Abhor all vice, in private as well as in publick, and look upon yourself as obliged to set good examples. Disdain all flattery . . . Do justice unto everybody and avoid partiality . . . I recommend unto you the highest love, affection and duty towards the King . . . Imitate his virtues, and look upon everything that is in opposition to that duty as destructive to yourself.

These were fine words: but did they mean anything to a child of his age? And, as such sentiments were echoed year after year, it is little wonder if the Prince tended to see in them no more significance than the offer of a customary greeting. By the time George was twelve years old the King was complaining to Holderness of his eldest son's duplicity and sly evasion, of his 'bad habit of not speaking the truth'.

Sometimes, of course, there was accord between father and son. 'Act uprightly and show the anxious care I have had of you has not been mispent', wrote the King in May 1778 from Portsmouth; and his son promptly replied, 'It shall always be the principal object of my life to deserve your Majesty's expressions of tenderness and affection'. But no flesh and blood Prince of Wales could be the paragon the King demanded and, as he passed from boyhood into adolescence, he abandoned the pretence of living up to his father's standards. In the summer of 1779 the Prince fell in love. Declaring himself with anticipatory relish, 'rather too fond of Wine and Women', he despatched sentimental letters to one of the young ladies at Court, Mary Hamilton, who was six years his senior and sufficiently sensible not to take the affair seriously. But, for the few friends who were around the Prince and knew his mind, the episode was a sign of imminent trouble. It came that autumn.

One of the sensations of the London season of 1779 was the performance of Mrs Mary Robinson, a remarkably beautiful actress of twenty-one, as Perdita in Garrick's modified version of *The Winter's Tale*. Accompanied by equerries and having sought permission from his father to attend the theatre, the Prince watched a performance and was infatuated by Perdita. They met secretly in the grounds of Kew, he gave her a locket with his portrait in miniature, and in time she gave him herself. The Prince wrote a delightfully ludicrous valedictory note to Mary Hamilton (*'Adieu, adieu, adieu, toujours chère.* Oh! Mrs Robinson') and began to pen indiscreetly endearing vows to his newest love. If she were Perdita then he would be Florizel, the son of King Polixenes in Shakespeare's play and the heroine's devoted lover; and it was thus that George signed himself in that rashly compromising correspondence.

It was, in many respects, an appropriate pen name. In those days the Prince of Wales possessed several external attributes of a theatrical idol. He was tall, floridly good looking and carried himself with dignity. Perdita Robinson herself was in later years to sigh wistfully for 'the grace of his person, the irresistible sweetness of his smile, the tenderness of his melodious yet manly voice'; and there are others who testify to his easy charm and agreeable company. At the time, however, Perdita – nobody thought of calling her by any other name – was at least as attracted by the gifts he showered on her, by the promise of future favours when he came of age, and by the status she thus acquired in the world of fashion: her pride and her loveliness still look down on us from the Gainsborough canvas in the Wallace Collection. The idyll could not last. By the spring of 1781 Florizel had tired of her but, unlike the accommodating Mary Hamilton, Perdita was reluctant to make her exit. The Prince of Wales found that, in this version of the tale, there was an epilogue which sullied the romantic purity of Shakespeare and Garrick. For Mrs Robinson had in her possession the Prince's letters and a bond of £20,000 to be paid in the autumn of 1783. Before the final curtain descended, George III had been righteously shocked by 'the shameful scrape' and had instructed Lord North (who had distant troubles of his own just then) to find £5,000 from the secret service funds for recovery of the Prince's reckless words. And in the Prince of Wales's accounts for 1787 we still see high on the list of 'pensions and annual donations' the item 'Mrs M. Robinson, £500'. Oh Mrs Robinson, indeed!

The episode confirmed George III in his darkest suspicions. Even before he learnt about Perdita, he had sent an oddly phrased reproach for his son's eighteenth birthday: 'Whilst you have been out of the sight of the world that has been kept under a veil by all those who cirrounded [sic] you, nay your foibles have been less perceived than I could have expected, yet your love of dissipation has for some months been with enough ill nature trumpeted in the public papers.' And at Christmas 1780 he proposed new arrangements for the Prince's way of life, which the King thought liberal and enlightened: continued residence at Buckingham House; sixteen horses ('I never had but three saddle horses'); the right to invite 'Lords, Grooms and Equerries' to private dinner parties in his apartments on Sundays and Thursdays, and to attend plays and operas 'provided you give me previous notice'; the opportunity to hold an occasional ball in the palace but never to attend dancing or assemblies in private houses, nor masquerades; and it would be expected that he should attend church on Sunday and all *levées* of the King, and accompany his father on his morning ride. It was, all in all, an impossibly strict regimen for a young man of naturally rebellious spirit; and by the following spring it had already broken down. On the first Thursday in May the Prince slipped out to Blackheath with two close friends (Anthony St Leger and Charles Wyndham) and there supped so well with Lord Chesterfield that he was 'indisposed', a fact which the King discovered and which received publicity in the *Morning Chronicle*. Once again a pained pen sent a regal reproof from one wing of Buckingham House to the other.

The antagonism between George III and his heir deepened in the following three years. This was in part a consequence of the Prince's wild behaviour, of that tedious iteration of drinking bouts and adventures of the heart which for so long was to ensure for him a bad press among historians. But other circumstances worsened the conflict of father and son. It was unfortunate that the Prince's emergence into society should coincide with a period of acute political rivalry and discontent within the governing circle. Throughout the first twenty years of George III's reign the Crown exercised unusual patronage in government, the King's Ministers being literally servants of his choice, like Bute (his old tutor) and Lord North, a man of equable temper and meritorious imperturbability. This system was abruptly shattered on 25 November 1781 when news reached the capital that, five weeks previously, Lord Cornwallis had surrendered Yorktown in Virginia to the American ex-colonists and their French allies. The City of London faced, for the first time since becoming a great financial centre, the unpleasant realities of a lost war and a discarded empire; and at Westminster the Whigs, long in opposition, sharpened their tongues and their memories of thirty years back; for in the first half of the century it had become accepted practice for politicians hopeful of future office to gather round the heir to the throne, creating 'a reversionary interest' which would challenge the established order, and clamber into office on the demise of the sovereign. This improvised counterbalance within the constitution now began once more to become active and, at nineteen, the Prince of Wales found himself, through no effort of his own, accepted as patron of the Opposition. It was an honorary status he maintained for almost three decades without seeking to acquire party management, or indeed any understanding of the internal stresses of politics.

The dangers of the Prince's position had been foreseen at the beginning of 1781 by his principal equerry and trusted friend, Colonel Gerard Lake, who before leaving for service in Virginia warned him against becoming a 'party man', and of allowing his 'great good nature . . . to be imposed upon by people who have not the smallest pretensions to your civility'. But the Prince found the attentions of the Whigs agreeable and it seemed natural to him that such sympathetic companions as Charles James Fox and Richard Brinsley Sheridan should share his life and interests. Nor is this surprising, for Fox's magical charm inspired friendship even among those who found his habits dissolute and, though Sheridan was often suspected of toadying, it would have been hard for the Prince to deny himself the company of the genius whose wit had created *The Rivals* when he was only twenty-three; for is there, perhaps, a touch of Anthony Absolute in the King's attempt to manage his son's life?

George III was dispirited by the constant sniping of the Whigs and by the gloomy news from America. He even went so far as to draft a message of abdication, but he stayed on, accepting for a few months in 1782 a Whig administration headed by the Marquess of Rockingham. Yet party loyalties and party labels meant little at this phase of constitutional development and by the following year there was a coalition, under the Whig Duke of Portland, of the Foxites and the discredited followers of Lord North (who had so recently been bitter enemies). It was this improbable alliance that was faced with the problem of the Prince of Wales's coming of age in August 1783. No one seriously expected he would remain living under his father's suspicious eye at Buckingham House (or, as it was more generally called then, 'The Queen's House'). He needed a separate establishment, a London residence of his own; and Fox and his friends pledged themselves to obtain for him a position of financial independence recognised by Parliament, though they were fully conscious that their own Whig principles dictated economy and retrenchment.

Two months before the Prince came of age, the Cabinet agreed that the heir to the throne might reasonably expect to receive £100,000 a year, of which £12,000 would come from the revenues of the Duchy of Cornwall and the rest from an annual grant approved by Parliament. At the same time the King would be asked to settle his son's outstanding debts, which had already shot up to £30,000, for the Prince was by nature inclined to expansive gestures of extravagance. But when, at the end of the second week in June, George III heard of these proposals he was 'filled with indignation and astonishment', to use his own words. As heir to the throne he had managed with half this allowance, and so had his father; and he could see no justification at a time when the taxation of his subjects was so high for 'a shameful squandering of public money' in order 'to gratify the passions of an ill-advised young man'. For a few days there was a strong possibility of the coalition breaking up over this question and the King would by no means have been sorry to see it go; but by the following week he had found a compromise, which would still leave him in reach of his son's purse-strings and, at the same time, not endear the Prince to members of the Commons. By this proposal, the Prince would receive

£62,000 a year of which £50,000 would come from the Civil List (i.e. from the King) and the remainder from the Duchy of Cornwall. Parliament would be asked to find £30,000 to settle his debts (a somewhat invidious request) and another £30,000 for fitting out Carlton House, a London royal residence only a few hundred yards east of St James's Palace and left neglected since the death there of George III's mother eleven years previously. Although Fox assured the Prince he was prepared to fight for the original proposal, the Prince did not wish to hold him to a pledge which he could hardly fulfil in the face of hostility from the Crown and most members of the administration; and on 22 June the Prince accepted the 'Establishment' recommended in the King's compromise.

There was, however, no real prospect of reconciliation between father and son. At the start of November the Prince moved into Carlton House and proceeded to take his seat in the House of Lords. A month later he voted for Fox's abortive India Bill, even though George III had made it clear to the Lords that he would regard anyone who supported the measure in the Upper House 'as an enemy'. The Prince's gesture of defiance was a sign of his continued attachment to the Foxites, but it could not save the Coalition. On 18 December 1783 George III dismissed his ministers. Next day he invited William Pitt (who was only three years older than the Prince of Wales) to become Prime Minister of a minority government. Every member of Pitt's Cabinet except himself was a peer, and no one rated highly the prospects of such a blue-blooded administration. They were wrong. Pitt remained at the head of affairs for the rest of the century; and 'the Prince's Friends' were left in querulous opposition.

It is hard to escape the feeling that the social world of the Opposition in the 1780s was infinitely more attractive to members of the ruling classes than any share in the cares of office. Transformation of Carlton House from a dilapidated mansion into a palace began in the autumn of 1783. The architect was Henry Holland, but it was the Prince who brought the fire of artistry to the project. His father had remarked that Carlton House only needed a touch of paint and 'handsome furniture where necessary' to make it a perfectly satisfactory home for his son. The Prince of Wales, however, prided himself on being a connoisseur of elegant living. He sought a building of solid assurance and exquisite detail; and his inspiration encompassed Corinthian porticos, an Ionic colonnade, and balustraded wings looking out on a garden in which there was a cascade, a temple paved in Italian marble, and disciplined lawns stretching beneath elms to the line of chestnuts along the Mall. Nor was this the limit of his vision. Later imagination added a Chinese salon hung with yellow silks, a 'hot bath' room, and a massive Gothic Conservatory opening on to the gardens. By the spring of 1784 Holland's work was sufficiently advanced for the Prince to welcome his friends to a ball, and on 19 May he held a fête in the gardens to celebrate Fox's personal electoral victory in his constituency of Westminster. It was a party which began with breakfast and ended in the early evening; and hundreds of Mr Pitt's opponents fortified their Whiggism in an encampment of marquees on the Prince's lawns. On that very Wednesday George III formally opened the new Parliamentary session, and as he rode in procession down the Mall he could not have failed to see the flutter of 'buff and blue' in his son's grounds. 'Buff and blue' were the electoral favours of the Foxites; but not so long ago they had been the colours of Washington's rebel army. There were occasions when the King found the Prince's lack of political inhibition a severe strain on his temper.

In the same summer the Prince made his first long visit to Brighton. He had been introduced briefly to the town in the previous September when he accompanied his uncle, the Duke of Cumberland, for a short recuperative course of sea-bathing – he suffered from swollen neck glands. In 1784 he leased Grove House, a pleasant red-brick building some six hundred yards from the sea, for ten weeks, and delighted in living a simple, if somewhat boisterous, existence on the Sussex coast. He went riding on the Downs and shooting partridges at Falmer, and he swam under the wary eye of a veteran bathing-machine attendant, 'Snoaker' John Miles, who had no intention of permitting his royal charge to get into difficulties and no hesitation in rebuking him for taking needless risk. But the Prince could not entirely escape the tensions of London; and on 26 July he undertook an exhausting journey which entitles him to be regarded as the founding father of South Coast commuting. Mounting his horse at five in the morning, he rode to London (reaching the capital at half-past nine), transacted his business, and rode back again to Brighton in the late afternoon, covering some one hundred and eighty miles that day with ten hours in the saddle. Weariness prevented him attending the ball in Shergold's Assembly Rooms that night, to the disappointment both of local worthies and of men of fashion who had been quick to seize on Brighton as a new centre for diversion.

On other days, however, his conviviality fulfilled all expectation. The little flint cobbled town – which had slept through so many centuries as Brighthelmstone – found itself merry with racing and shooting parties, with long hours of drinking and giddy flirtations, and with all the exciting uncertainty of wagers on improbable feats. The Prince liked Brighton; and Brighton, for the most part, liked the Prince. Once the annual migration to Sussex was established in his personal calendar, he sought a permanent residence, but it was only on his fourth visit that he decided to employ Henry Holland on converting an old farm-house into his Pavilion by the sea, and not until 1787 did he move into the partially refurbished building. By then, however, the name of Brighton was already so closely associated with the Prince of Wales that the town acquired a European reputation; and so it was to continue for more than forty years.

The reckless exhilaration of life at Carlton House and in Brighton encouraged rather than diminished the Prince's vitality; and experience had not destroyed his desire to play the role of Florizel. There was a romance with Lady Melbourne (who, with a happy instinct for apt rewards, had her husband created a Gentleman of the Bedchamber to the Prince of Wales) and a sad entanglement with the over-amorous wife of Karl von Hardenberg, later Prussian Foreign Minister and in due course honoured by George IV as one of Europe's liberators. But in the spring of 1784 the Prince met a highly respectable and (as he thought) pleasantly amiable widow of twenty-eight, Mrs Fitzherbert; and, to the consternation of his Foxite friends, within a few weeks he was anxious to make her his wife. To such a step there were three objections: the least serious was that she had been born a commoner, Maria Smythe; more awkward was the Royal Marriage Act of 1772, which invalidated any marriage by a member of the royal family under the age of twenty-five contracted without the King's consent; and gravest obstacle of all was Mrs Fitzherbert's Roman Catholic faith, for under the Act of Settlement of 1701 no Prince who married a 'Papist' might succeed to the throne.

Mrs Fitzherbert differed in character and physique from his earlier loves. Although she undoubtedly felt a sincere and enduring affection for the Prince, she was no romantic and her religious scruples held her inclinations in restraint so that she would never be content to live as the Prince's mistress. He, however, was infatuated with her, though the ample figure and aquiline nose of her portraits makes one assume her charm lay in a serene disposition rather than in her person. In June 1784 he tried to make her relent by a dramatically contrived scene in Carlton House in which he appeared to have stabbed himself: she accepted a ring from him and promptly crossed to France, either in flight or with the intention that the Prince would join her for a secret marriage. Certainly the Prince requested permission from George III to live abroad, rather strangely giving as his reason a desire to economise; and he received a firm refusal from his father. There was some wild talk, over the cups of his Whig friends, of selling his jewels and seeking a new life with Maria in the glorious freedom of the Americas. Fox was sufficiently alarmed to beg the Prince to give up all thoughts of matrimony with Mrs Fitzherbert and was reassured by the firm reply he received. And yet, before writing to his 'dear Charles', the Prince had already taken steps to overcome her reluctance. On 3 November 1785 he despatched to France a letter of more than six thousand words: he begged 'Maria my beloved wife (for such you really are)' to return to England; and he told her of how he was resisting all proposals to marry him to any foreign princesses, and of his plans for a secret wedding once she was back in London.

She returned to her house in Park Street, Mayfair, a month later. An Anglican priest, the Reverend Robert Butt, sometime Vicar of Twickenham, was released from the debtors' prison on payment of £500 to settle his liabilities (which were considerably less than those of his sponsor). He agreed to perform a marriage ceremony according to the rites of the Church of England and was promised a bishopric when the Prince came into his own, a pledge which the unexpected longevity of George III made it impossible to fulfil. On the evening of 15 December 1785 the Prince and Mrs Fitzherbert were secretly married at her house, with the bride's uncle and brother as witnesses. Husband and wife in the sight of God, though not by the law of the realm, George and Maria drove off that night for a brief honeymoon at Ormeley Lodge on Ham Common in Surrey. The shafts of their carriage are said to have snapped during the ten-mile journey.

2

Debts and Disappointments
1785–96

The secret was surprisingly well kept. It is true that during the Christmas and New Year festivities there was speculation that Maria Fitzherbert would shortly be created a Duchess and move into a wing of Carlton House; and a few gossips even mentioned a mysterious Catholic priest who had allegedly officiated at some clandestine ceremony; but all such talk was discounted by the Prince's political allies. They could not believe he would have acted so foolishly after his recent assurances to Fox, and, with Mrs Fitzherbert living in quiet domesticity in Park Street and the Prince's habits comfortingly familiar, it seemed as if the rumours were groundless. Only a handful of upper-crust Catholic families and Tory back-benchers continued to give them credence.

Yet the chronic financial difficulties of the Prince made it impossible for him to conceal all his private concerns from the public eye, and there are times when he seems to have had little wish to do so. His debts mounted rapidly until, at the end of April 1786, he was forced to send an abjectly embarrassing request to his father for assistance in 'the very difficult situation I find myself in'. Not unreasonably, George III demanded a full written statement of the Prince's liabilities and some guarantee that future expenditure would be contained within the annual sum granted him in 1783. On 15 June the Prince accordingly sent his father a brief 'statement of arrears', in which he listed only debts contracted up to the end of the previous March: the total sum amounted to £269,878:6s:7¼d, of which nearly a third was for Carlton House alone. The King was displeased and unco-operative: he complained that the items listed were insufficiently explained and that there was still no assurance the prodigal would mend his ways. His father's lack of sympathy stung the Prince into drastic action. In the first week of July 1786 he shut down Carlton House, dismissed his servants, trimmed the size of his Household, and sold his stud and most of his carriages. He was determined to show his father and his critics that he could follow a simple life as a private person. It must be admitted that princely austerity was not rigorously ascetic: it involved hiring a public chaise and trundling down to Brighton for three months with Mrs Fitzherbert; but his gestures of economy were sufficiently dramatic to draw attention to his plight.

Rather unexpectedly, the King's attitude produced a reaction which seemed to swing public feeling in the Prince's favour; and at the start of 1787 the Foxites thought the Prince might reasonably seek Parliamentary support for his financial relief. One of the representatives of the City of London gave notice that on 4 May he would seek to move an address to the King for 'measures . . . to rescue' his son 'from his present embarrassments', and the Prince personally began to canvass members of the House. But, on 3 May, Pitt approached the Prince and let him know of the King's willingness to assist him, although it was assumed that from gratitude the Prince would no longer be such an active political partisan. A full-scale debate on the financial difficulties of the heir to the throne was therefore avoided at the last minute; but there were exchanges between Buckingham House and Carlton House for more than a fortnight before a compromise was reached. The King agreed to allow his son an additional £10,000 a year from the Civil List; and the Pitt administration undertook to recommend Parliament to settle the Prince's immediate debts, which proper accountancy had shown to be less than he had indicated in the earlier correspondence with his father. The Commons duly voted him £160,000 for payment of liabilities and an additional £60,000 for completion of work on Carlton House. In return for these generous sums the Prince gave the King an undertaking 'never to incur future debts, which must undoubtedly be as disagreeable to the King as painful to himself'. At the beginning of June 1787 there was an outward reconciliation between the King and his son. Carlton House was re-opened and most of the Prince's Household reinstated.

The 'unpleasant business' raised indirectly an awkward problem. During the discussions in the Commons John Rolle, a sturdy Devonian Tory, asked members to take note of 'a question which might affect both Church and State'; and it was commonly assumed that Rolle was thus introducing into the records of the House an oblique allusion to the reported marriage of the Prince and Mrs Fitzherbert. Fox at once seized the opportunity to declare vigorously that such a union 'could have never happened legally' and, indeed, 'never did happen in any way whatsoever'. No doubt Fox sincerely believed he was speaking the truth, for he had confidence in the Prince's denials given to him four days before the secret ceremony. Maria Fitzherbert was, however, indignant that no one in the House had thought of defending her own honour; and the Prince on her behalf induced Sheridan on the following day to make a speech in which, without mentioning names, he referred to a lady whose character 'was entitled to the truest and most general respect' and 'on whose conduct truth could fix no just reproach'. It is not clear if, at the time, the Prince let Sheridan know of his true relationship with Maria nor if he mentioned it to Charles Grey, the most prominent of Fox's younger followers; but it would appear that Fox was informed of it by one of Mrs Fitzherbert's family when next he went to Brooks's Club, and that he decided not to create a constitutional crisis by seeking to modify what he had already said in the House. Relations between Fox and the Prince were a shade less cordial for some months although there was never a complete break, as some writers have said. The Prince still consulted the Whig leader over his financial situation. Mrs Fitzherbert, on the other hand, continued to treat Fox coldly.

It is unlikely that George III knew – or had any wish to know – of the precise relationship between his eldest son and Mrs Fitzherbert. The poor man was disappointed in his children: even his favourite son, the Duke of York (who returned to England from Hanover in 1787), was constantly at the gaming tables, with remarkable lack of success; and the King blamed the Prince of Wales for initiating the Duke into the vices of London Society. By the spring of 1788 George III was in low spirits and failed to respond to his physicians' treatment; and in July they packed him off for a rare holiday in Cheltenham where they hoped the waters would relieve the bilious disorders from which he appeared to be suffering. His behaviour was mildly eccentric, notably during a visit to Worcester where he roused the Dean from his sleep so that he could watch the light of dawn flood the cathedral nave. He returned to Kew refreshed in September and it was not until the end of October that it was suspected he was suffering from mental disorders.

On 1 November, he was well enough to go hunting at Windsor, though both the Prince of Wales and the Duke of York were summoned to Court. Once they arrived, it was impossible to keep the King's illness a secret; and by 5 November it was rumoured among Ministers and Opposition at Westminster that his life was in peril, wretchedly fading away through nights of sleepless delirium. The Prince of Wales, magnificently dressed and resplendent with orders of chivalry, sat waiting for news of his accession; or so it was said.

Such tales were much exaggerated. Physically George III was strong, and by the middle of the month he was out of danger. His mental confusion, however, remained intense and sometimes it was necessary to use coercion in order to restrain his gusts of passion. At the end of November he was well enough to be moved from Windsor to Kew, where doctors could attend him more conveniently and where it was easier for members of the Court and the Government to discover details of his condition from day to day. Throughout England there was a marked sentiment of affectionate regard, and almost of understanding, for a sovereign whose qualities had in the past rarely stirred the enthusiasm of his subjects; and, at Versailles, both Louis XVI and Marie Antoinette shed tears of sympathy when the British ambassador told them of his King's sufferings. But in London the tragedy of the monarch's wandering mind was often forgotten in the sheer excitement of political uncertainty. Clearly, if the King could not exercise his powers, there was need for a Regency, and for this dignity there was no natural candidate other than the Prince of Wales. But it was assumed, even by the Prime Minister, that once the royal prerogative of creating Ministers passed into the Prince's hands, the days of Pitt's administration would be numbered. The Whigs stood on the threshold of office; and they began to draw up possible lists of Ministers. It was a fascinating game and the Prince himself was a willing participant, on one occasion leaving Sheridan with high expectations of receiving the Exchequer. But there were other problems for His Royal Highness to consider. Should he promote all his brothers to the rank of Field-Marshal, or retain the distinction for himself? What title might Mrs Fitzherbert bear if he made her a Duchess? What style and inscription should be placed on the Regency Medals which, a little unfeelingly, it was proposed to strike for the occasion? No one doubted that, by the spring of 1789, England would be governed by the 'Prince's Friends';

26

and to the Buff and Blues such a revolution seemed worthy of com-memoration in advance.

There were three reasons why the government did not change. The most important of these was that the King's mental disorder proved shorter in duration than earlier reports suggested, and he had officially recovered his health by the last week in February. There might, never-theless, have been a Whig administration during the final two months of his illness had it not been for the skill with which Pitt delayed passage of an Act of Regency and, by contrast, the disastrous tactical blunders of Fox. For the Whig leader put forward the supremely un-Whiggish doctrine that a Regency was the Prince's by right and was not depen-dent on any restrictions of Parliament. The whole question of the Prince's powers was thus made the subject of long debate in the Commons; and inevitably discussion strayed into other aspects of his life. His extravagance over the new Royal Pavilion at Brighton revived old complaints; and the egregious Mr Rolle was once more ready to make mischief by innuendo 'with respect to a certain lady'. It was not difficult to show Pitt as a friend of the people; and to discredit both Fox and his patron, the Prince. The Press was, for the most part, on the side of Pitt; and uninhibited newspapers, like the recently estab-lished *Times*, did not hesitate to attack the heir to the throne as 'an English Prince who shows a predilection for foreigners' and saw the shadows of a Papist cabal in his attempts to enlist support from un-committed waverers in both the Lords and Commons. Although much that was written remained scurrilous, with caricature savagely distort-ing attitudes and opinions, there was enough clumsy stupidity in the Prince's political behaviour for most of the attacks to be justified; and he became increasingly unpopular, especially in London. One evening that March his carriage was blocked by an excited mob who called on him to shout 'Pitt for ever'. They met a sharp response: 'Damn Pitt!', he yelled, 'Fox for ever!'; and his coach clattered on down the Hay-market to the theatre.

He could still win a cheer at Brighton, or in some of the areas tradi-tionally at variance with the opinions of the capital. Thus in August 1789, while his father was enjoying sea-bathing at Weymouth, the Prince visited York and was rapturously welcomed by its predominantly Whig voters. In general, however, his reputation remained low through-out the four years which followed the Regency Crisis. The frustration

27

with which he had seen power suddenly taken from him by his father's recovery led him to double his devotion to drink, gambling and women; and his temper was made no easier by his father's assertion that, had the Regency ever been formally established by Parliament, he would not have resumed sovereign authority on his recovery. Neither the Prince nor the Duke of York found it easy to hide their chagrin, and often did not bother to try. When, on St George's Day 1789, the royal family attended a service of thanksgiving in St Paul's Cathedral for the King's return to normal health, both his eldest sons behaved disgracefully, ostentatiously chewing biscuits during Archbishop Moore's address. The Prince remained bitter towards Pitt and towards the Queen, who was herself angry with the intrigues of her two sons during their father's illness. Most of the newspapers continued to thunder their indignation: the Prince of Wales, commented *The Times* in one of its less vituperative moods, was 'like a man . . . who at all times would prefer a girl and a bottle to politics and a sermon'. So, no doubt, did most of his future subjects; but they expected greater dignity from the heir to the throne, and they branded his actions as unfilial. The scorn with which the Prince was ridiculed in these years pursued him to the grave and beyond.

Yet it is possible to feel some sympathy for the Prince. Although the most intelligent of the King's sons, he was deliberately excluded from the world of politics and, unlike his brothers, never trained as a soldier or sailor. He pursued pleasure partly from inclinations of character but also because there was little enough else for him to do. His brothers had all travelled on the Continent, where new doctrines were beginning to challenge the whole concept of monarchy. His own itinerary was confined to a smaller area: York, for the races, in the North; Newmarket (more racing) in the East; Bath, for the art of living, in the West; and Brighton, for the delight of being himself, in the South. There, on the Sussex coast, he passed the summer of 1791 in a newly found enthusiasm for the 'manly exercise' of cricket, a sport in which he showed no aptitude with the bat although surprising agility in the field; but he was not ignorant of what was happening across the Channel and, in the following year, personally welcomed parties of French refugees as they arrived on Brighton beach to escape the Jacobin wrath. His printed correspondence shows how deeply their plight affected him. Many of the aristocrats who perished in the

Terror were acquaintances and several had been his guests in Sussex or in London in happier times. He was especially shocked by the fate of the Princesse de Lamballe, hideously butchered in the September massacres of 1792, almost five years to the day since she had stood beside the Prince and Mrs Fitzherbert at Brighton Races. On the other hand, he was so thrilled by the escape of the Comtesse de Noailles and her child that he immediately sent off a three-thousand-word letter to his mother in Weymouth with details of all the Comtesse had told him: she had got away from Dieppe disguised as a boy sailor in the Brighton packet boat, and was still wearing a seaman's jacket when she reached the shores of Sussex.

The Prince's hatred of 'the damnable doctrines of the hell-begotten Jacobines' – the phrase comes from another letter he wrote to the Queen, on 24 September – dampened his enthusiasm for the Foxites, though he remained personally attached to their leader. Four months previously the Prince had caused considerable surprise by an apparently spontaneous maiden speech in the House of Lords in which he supported a proclamation against seditious writings while declaring his devotion to the existing form of the constitution. Although he only spoke for three minutes, his words were warmly received and won widespread approval, even in *The Times*. They helped to ease relations with the King and Queen and he was once again welcomed to Windsor and, later in the year, to Weymouth. It is possible that the Prince's willingness for a family reconciliation was connected with his debts which, despite his earlier pledges of economy, stood at almost £400,000 at the time he made his maiden speech. But the King, though sympathetic, was unforthcoming; and Pitt had no intention of squeezing more money out of Parliament. Once again the Prince announced that he would economise, drastically reducing his establishment and postponing embarrassing settlements by a loan negotiated in the Netherlands. He put aside ideas, with which he had amused himself at Brighton, for transforming the Pavilion into a palace no less remarkable than Carlton House. At the age of thirty he announced he had withdrawn into 'complete retirement'.

But in that winter of 1792–3 the European situation rapidly deteriorated. Early in February the French Republic declared war on Britain; and the Prince longed for action. He was commissioned as Colonel in command of the Tenth Light Dragoons ('the Prince of Wales's Own') by the King, and the appointment filled him with childish delight. A few days later, looking disturbingly gross in a tight-fitting uniform, the Prince rode beside his father down the Mall to the Horse Guards to inspect an advance party of the expeditionary force setting out for Holland at the start of twenty years of fighting. The Duke of York crossed with them to take command of the British forces in the Low Countries – or, as the cynics said, to avoid his creditors – and the Prince declared that he would willingly have served under his brother, but it was not felt desirable for the two eldest sons of the King of England to pit their talents against the French.

For most of the year 1793 the Prince took his military duties very seriously. In midsummer he wrote to Coburg (the allied generalissimo in Flanders) and to the Austrian Emperor offering his services, though nothing came of this gesture beyond a civil exchange of courtesies. The Prince was accordingly left to soldier on with the Light Dragoons; and on 3 August he rode at the head of his regiment through the sleepy town of Lewes to establish a camp at Hove – where, oddly enough, he was actually as near the enemy capital as the Duke of York or any other princely commander in the field. For more than a month the Prince of Wales conducted military exercises and manœuvres with his men on the South Downs; and at the end of these exertions he was disappointed not to be promoted to the rank of full general. It would be misleading to assume that, during these weeks, he suffered the full privations of a campaigner; for the colonel's tent was a large marquee emblazoned with the Prince of Wales's feathers and containing a huge divan (draped in lilac and green chintz) and chairs costing over £1,000. Moreover the Light Dragoons were rarely more than two hours' ride from the Royal Pavilion. But at least the Prince became acquainted with the problems of marches and counter-marches, though his enthusiasm for soldiering died away with the rains of autumn and he was back in Carlton House by mid-September. For the rest of his life he retained detailed knowledge of uniforms and parade punctilio. It could, indeed, be said that over such matters he showed greater expertise than young Colonel Bonaparte (who was busy just then with grape-shot against British marines in Toulon).

Though much in the Prince's character remained pathetically ridiculous, he was becoming far more conscious of his responsibilities, and at thirty-one had at last outgrown adolescence. Some years before, he let it be known he would never marry a foreign princess or have legitimate children to succeed to the throne; such matters, he indicated, might be left to the Duke of York. But in the winter of 1793–4 he began to change his ideas. He was still fond of Mrs Fitzherbert, although he complained that her temper strained their good relations. Now, however, she could no longer claim first place among his female companions. He was infatuated with the Countess of Jersey, a well-proportioned grandmother nine years older than himself. It is possible that Lady Jersey, who was a friend of his mother, was never physically the Prince's mistress and that he was attracted as much by her vivacity and good humour as by her person. Gossip, of course, maligned her; and it was widely said she was eager for the Prince to break with Maria Fitzherbert and conclude an official marriage in the belief that she could dominate any princess whom he might take as a wife. Yet such deep subtlety on the part of Lady Jersey is improbable, and out of character: she was the type of woman who might contrive a momentary triumph but who lacked the persistence to plan far ahead. There are less coquettish reasons for the Prince's behaviour, chief among them the nagging problem of his debts (which was now worsened by the high rates of interest he was called on to pay). A good marriage, and the prospect of an heir to the throne, might induce Parliament to grant him another £50,000 a year.

There were few eligible royal brides. Some months before he might have had the good fortune to marry the lovely and courageous Louise of Mecklenburg-Strelitz, but she had become Crown-Princess of Prussia, and he turned instead to Princess Caroline of Brunswick, youngest daughter of George III's elder sister. The Prince of Wales had never met his cousin, but the Duke of York had already written warmly of the hospitality he received at the Court of Brunswick and everyone in the royal family seemed to approve of the marriage, except Queen Charlotte who had never thought much of the Brunswicks. The Prince himself had an exaggerated respect for the fighting traditions of the dynasty. The strange contradictions in the Prince's psychology still made him delight in anything soldierly and may have inclined him to look more favourably on a bride from Brunswick than on one from any of the other German states.

In November 1794 the Earl of Malmesbury (a distinguished diplomat

who, as Sir James Harris, had long served the Prince before his eleva-
tion to the peerage) was sent across to Germany with instructions to
arrange the marriage and to bring back the bride to England. He was
not supposed to exercise any discretion over the desirability of the
marriage but merely to complete the legal formalities. It cannot have
been a pleasant mission for Malmesbury. His journal shows that he
found Caroline, at twenty-six, stockily built and with little to her credit
except a fine head of hair. She dressed dowdily, spoke too much and
too coarsely, lacked moral reticence or good sense, and washed so little
that the Earl found her presence malodorous. He gave no warning of
these faults to the Prince but, accompanied by Caroline, he set out by a
circuitous route to avoid the French armies and landed at Greenwich
on 5 April 1795. The Prince, rather strangely, did not come to greet
Caroline himself. She was escorted into London by a detachment of
the Light Dragoons and by a lady of the Bedchamber recently assigned
to the Princess by Queen Charlotte, the Countess of Jersey. Caroline
had already heard much to Lady Jersey's discredit: and to be met by
the bridegroom's apparent mistress rather than by the bridegroom was
an inauspicious welcome to England.

Princess Caroline arrived at St James's Palace in the early afternoon
and the Prince of Wales came to visit her soon after. It was hardly an
instance of love at first sight. 'Harris, I am not well,' said the Prince to
Malmesbury as soon as he had greeted Caroline. 'Pray get me a glass of
brandy.' And after he had left the room, poor Caroline turned to Malmesbury and complained, 'I find him very stout and by no means as
handsome as his portrait.' Malmesbury, who although conscious of
Caroline's failings was sympathetically inclined towards her, held out
hopes of growing understanding on deeper acquaintance; but it was
soon clear that the Prince could not endure Caroline's company unless
he was well fortified with alcohol. They were married on the evening
of 8 April 1795 in the Chapel Royal at St James's Palace. The ceremony
was well-staged: a candle-lit altar; a special anthem of rejoicing;
trumpet fanfares; and throughout the land church bells pealing across
the spring-time countryside. It was a pity the bridegroom was drunk.
Not since the marriage of Henry viii and Anne of Cleves had an English
prince approached his nuptial bed with such antipathy.

The Prince soon received another disappointment. He had assumed
that, if he married, Pitt would advise Parliament to settle all his debts

1 (*above*) Painting by Zoffany of Queen Charlotte with her two eldest sons, George, Prince of Wales, and Frederick, Duke of York.

2 (*left*) George III as a young man. Portrait by Gainsborough Dupont.

3 Thomas Gainsborough was commissioned by George III to paint the portraits of the King, Queen and their thirteen children. These were executed at Windsor in 1782. The Prince of Wales is represented in the central miniature of the top row.

4 (*left*) George painted as Prince of Wales by Matthew Brown in about 1790.

5 (*right*) Mrs Mary Robinson, who became known as Perdita through her performance in *The Winter's Tale* in London in 1779. She became George's first mistress, and earned him the nickname of Florizel. Portrait by Gainsborough.

6 (*left*) David Garrick, as both actor and theatre manager, was responsible for reviving interest in Shakespeare's plays. He produced over twenty four of Shakespeare's plays at his theatre in Drury Lane and played the leading role in most of them. In this engraving, Garrick is shown as Macbeth.

7 (*below*) Garrick died in 1779, but the traditions that he had established were continued by Edmund Kean during the 1790s and early 1800s. Here he is depicted playing Richard iii before the Prince Regent.

Carlton House was re-modelled for the Prince of Wales by Henry Holland in 1783. The two engravings shown here are taken from W. H. Pine's *History of the Royal Residences,* 1819. 8 (*above*) The façade on the Mall, with its huge Corinthian portico. 9 (*left*) The Gothic Conservatory, which was to provide George with the setting for many of his exotic parties.

10 (*above*) In 1784, the Prince of Wales paid his first visit to Brighton, where he leased a farm house. Three years later, he commissioned Henry Holland to convert the farm house into his Pavilion by the sea. This engraving shows Henry Holland's design for the Pavilion.

11 (*below*) The Duke of York's bedroom at the Brighton Pavilion, which has now been furnished to represent a drawing-room.   The Hepplewhite furniture belonged to Mrs Fitzherbert, from her house on the Steine.   The simple style of the room reflects the character of Holland's Pavilion, before Nash's exotic alterations.

12 (*above*) The Prince of Wales was married in secret to Mrs Fitzherbert on 15 December 1785. This contemporary caricature depicts Charles James Fox holding Mrs Fitzherbert's left hand, while Lord North is sitting fast asleep.

13 (*below*) The marriage of the Prince of Wales and Princess Caroline of Brunswick, which took place in the Chapel Royal at St James's Palace on 8 April 1795. Painting by Singleton.

14 (*above*) Allegorical design by West for a Regency Bill. In the event, George III recovered and the Prince of Wales did not become Regent until 1811.

15 (*below left*) William Pitt the Younger, who by skilled tactics delayed passage of the Act of Regency for two months, until the King was able to recover from his illness. Portrait by Thomas Lawrence.

16 (*below right*) Richard Brinsley Sheridan, playwright, Whig politician and friend of the Prince of Wales. His career in Parliament was not at all successful, although in 1788 he had high hopes of receiving the Exchequer in the event of a Regency.

George enjoyed riding throughout his life, although his increasing corpulence precluded him from any violent exercise. After 1791 he no longer raced horses under his own colours, following an unfortunate incident at Newmarket, but he frequently attended race-meetings and betted heavily. 17 (*above*) The Prince driving to Ascot 'with a lady of quality'. 18 (*below*) The Prince at Newmarket.

19 Frances Countess of Jersey. By 1794 she had become the favourite companion of the Prince of Wales, and her presence in the royal household represented a considerable annoyance for Princess Caroline when she arrived in England.

20 George came under heavy attack from the Press and cartoonists in the 1790s for his extravagance and loose-living. This cartoon by Gillray shows 'A Voluptuary under the Horrors of Digestion' and makes allusion to his relationship with the Roman Catholic Mrs Fitzherbert.

21 On 7 January 1796, Princess Charlotte was born. This engraving shows Princess Charlotte with the Princess of Wales in 1798.

22 Gillray's cartoon of Pitt's proposal to create legislative union between England and Ireland by transferring the Irish Parliament from Dublin to Westminster. This proposal was vetoed by George III, who refused to accept the measure of Catholic Emancipation contained in the Act, and Pitt's Government fell.

23 A political cartoon showing Lady Hertford, urged on by Lord Yarmouth, cutting off the Prince of Wales's locks. The locks are intended to represent 'the Prince's friends', Holland, Sheridan, Grenville and Grey, being separated from the Prince by the Tory Lady Hertford.

The brothers of the Prince of Wales. 24 (*top left*) Edward, Duke of Kent, 1818, by Sir William Beechey. 25 (*top right*) Ernest Augustus, Duke of Cumberland by George Dawe. 26 (*above left*) Augustus Frederick, Duke of Sussex, 1789, by Guy Head. 27 (*above right*) Adolphus, Duke of Cambridge.

28 (*top left*) William Duke of Clarence, who later became William IV. Pencil drawing by Sir George Hayter.

29 (*top right*) Frederick, Duke of York, George III's second and favourite son. Painting by David Wilkie.

30 (*above*) A cartoon by Cruikshank, published in 1811. This alludes to the scandal in which Mary Anne Clarke, the Duke of York's mistress, was discovered to have acted as broker in the sale of military commissions and promotions. The Duke of York is depicted in the centre dressed as commander-in-chief of the army, while Mary Anne Clarke is shown on the far left.

31 Cartoon by Gillray, showing Mrs Fitzherbert with Minnie Seymour, being carried up to heaven. This is a Protestant protest against Minnie being brought up by a Roman Catholic.

so that he might begin life with England's future Queen-Consort unencumbered by past follies. In 1795 it was, after all, a full eight years since Parliament had last paid off his liabilities and since then he had incurred new obligations which meant that when he married he owed £630,000. It is difficult to see how a man whose patriotism was genuinely stirred by the war with France could possibly have thought the House of Commons would throw a personal burden of this nature on the tax-payer at such a time. Naturally most people believed that the Prince's debts could be attributed to reckless living, to wine and women and dicing. In fact, though much money was wasted on pleasures of the moment, most of his debts sprang from his desire to build up a collection of artistic treasures which were in time to prove a monetary investment as well as a contribution to the cultural heritage of the nation. But it is unreasonable to expect that the Commons would have appreciated the Prince's far-sightedness in a country deep in war and agrarian distress and, though Pitt was prepared to recommend an increase in the Prince's annual income, he knew that his Government would have fallen if he had sought total settlement of the Prince's liabilities. As it was, the Commons insisted on setting aside some £65,000 a year (together with the revenues of the Duchy of Cornwall for the next quarter of a century) in debt redemption; and, at the same time, they secured the appointment of Parliamentary commissioners to administer his debts. In the end the Prince, thoroughly dissatisfied, was left with a nominal income of £60,000 a year, which was less than the Establishment he had received as a bachelor of twenty-one. Discussion of the Prince's apparently spendthrift habits in Parliament inevitably led to another strong wave of hostility among the general public, who on this occasion did not spare other members of the royal family, including to some extent the King. It was, all in all, an unhappy episode.

So, too, was the marriage itself. At the time it was widely believed among the aristocracy that the Prince and Princess of Wales lived as man and wife for only the briefest moment. The marriage was rapidly consummated and a child, Princess Charlotte, was duly born on 7 January 1796, almost precisely nine months after the wedding ceremony. Yet by the spring of that year the Prince and Princess were virtually separated, maintaining in effect two households and rarely speaking to each other. Perhaps an arrangement of this kind was inevitable, given the difference in temperament which each perceived as soon as they met. But some of the letters in the printed edition of the Prince's correspondence suggest that their mutual repugnance in the first few months of marriage was never so intense as they later led their respective friends to believe. Twice at midsummer the Prince wrote to his mother assuring her of Caroline's good health and high spirits and of the pleasure she was gaining from residence in Brighton. There is no reason why the Prince should have troubled to dissimulate in correspondence with the Queen, for she had never liked the Brunswick marriage and had known of her son's disappointment on meeting Caroline almost as soon as he swallowed that first brandy. Moreover, on several occasions during the summer the Prince's favourite sister, Elizabeth, wrote affectionately about Caroline to her brother, once adding the hopeful comment that she was sure, 'You will have her turn into a very comfortable little wife'. But it could not be. He had beside him Lady Jersey, a woman totally different in intellect and bearing from Caroline; and, as the winter months brought round once more the anniversary of his secret marriage, the thought of the woman from whom he had deliberately cut himself off seems to have stirred his mind. In the week of Princess Charlotte's birth he was, quite clearly, in a state of intense nervous depression.

The child was born on a Thursday morning. The Prince had spent Tuesday and Wednesday nights without sleep. On Friday and Saturday he wrote perfectly calm letters in which he let the family know about the health of Caroline and of his own satisfaction at the birth of 'the little girl'. He even received a letter from his sister Elizabeth, in which she said, 'Thank God that you are now happy'. Whether or not this phrase momentarily unhinged him, we do not know; but on Sunday he wrote an extraordinarily long 'last will and testament' in which all his suppressed anger with Caroline seems to have boiled over. 'To her who is called the Princess of Wales I leave one shilling,' he wrote. His chief concern, after safe-guarding 'my infant daughter', was with 'my Maria Fitzherbert who is my wife in the eyes of God, and who is and ever will be such in mine'; and he begged that on his death 'the picture of my beloved wife, my Maria Fitzherbert, may be interred with me'. It is a tragically sad document, so filled with presentiment of imminent death that it reads as if he were contemplating taking his own life. Outwardly he seems to have recovered from his despondency by the end of the month; but, significantly, the 'last will and testament' was not destroyed. It even passed eventually into the hands of Mrs Fitz-herbert. So long as the Prince preserved a document written at a time of hysterical depression, there was never any hope that the baby would grow up within the comfort of parental understanding. Carlton House was no place for a royal nursery.

3
The Fiend 1796–1807

Rumours of a breakdown in the Prince's marriage began to excite comment in fashionable London drawing-rooms early in March 1796. As if to give the lie to social gossip, husband and wife went to the opera together on Tuesday, 15 March, and were observed to be on terms of almost affectionate cordiality. But on Friday in that same week the Prince sent for 'Harris' (Lord Malmesbury) and discussed with him ways in which it might be possible for the Princess to be given a separate establishment, an arrangement to which Caroline had apparently consented several months previously. Poor Malmesbury, hopelessly confused by the Prince's elaborate verbiage, thought he intended to seek a formal ending of the marriage and begged him not to risk hostile demonstrations by taking such a drastic step. The Prince, however, explained that so long as Caroline made no 'attempt to give false impressions of me to the public and to raise herself at my expense', he had no desire for his domestic difficulties to be generally noised abroad. They would, he assumed, continue to reside in Carlton House although they would only meet on formal occasions. They could keep in touch with each other by an exchange of notes when necessary: this was, after all, a regular method of communication between the King and the Prince when he had been expected to live at Buckingham House, and he could see no reason why it should not now provide the means of contact with his consort. On 30 April he defined, in a letter to Caroline, the terms on which they might maintain 'tranquil and comfortable society' by avoiding each other's company. He hoped that 'the rest of our lives will be passed in uninterrupted tranquility'.

There was never the slightest prospect of Caroline meekly accepting such a humiliating contract, even though she let her husband know of the patient resignation with which she had received his message. To the Prince's fury she insisted on raising the whole matter with the King, and she continued to complain at the indignities thrust upon her by the retention of the Countess of Jersey in her household. Nor did she limit her protests to the family circle. In character she was no less exhibitionist than her husband and she enjoyed pouring out her woes to a group of men who seem to have felt for her none of the repugnance she aroused in the Prince. By 24 May her plight had stirred the heart of the editor of *The Times*, who always enjoyed using his columns to snipe at her husband, and when four days later she made a visit to the opera the audience rose to its feet and applauded her. A second evening at the opera on 31 May led to another round of public acclamation, sweet music to Caroline's ears. Her husband retired to Surrey and dashed off indignant letters to his father and mother: 'I am serving my family in the most essential manner by ridding them of a fiend under whose influence otherwise, not only I, but you and all the rest of us must make up our minds to submit to for the whole of our lives,' he wrote to the Queen on 4 June. Such deep detestation of his wife almost unhinged his sanity.

Caroline won from the Prince far more concessions than he had ever intended. Lady Jersey was permitted to resign, and the Princess herself was allowed to leave Carlton House and set up her own establishment in the Thames-side village of Charlton. For two years she leased the local rectory; but in 1798 George III, who retained some affection for his niece and daughter-in-law, appointed her Ranger of Greenwich Park, and she was able to move into the more spacious dignity of Montague House, Blackheath. Occasionally Caroline would come up to Carlton House for ceremonial functions or to see Princess Charlotte; but for most of the year she remained in her Kentish retreat. It was, in many ways, a pleasant existence. She had lessons in playing the harp, in speaking English, and in painting. At Blackheath she had her own vegetable garden, from which she would sell produce at Covent Garden market. There were charitable causes in which she could interest herself, and she was a kindly patron for the orphan boys and girls from the dockyard townships along the river. She had agreeable neighbours: Mr Spencer Perceval, a rising Tory MP, lived in Greenwich; young George Canning called; and there was a diverting cluster of naval officers, from the septuagenarian Admiral Lord Hood, whose ensign had so recently fluttered in Toulon and Ajaccio, down to mere captains of frigates with reputations yet to be made. The Princess soon established an embryo court around her. Occasionally its pursuits were rowdily boisterous and frequently they were indiscreet. Sometimes, too, it had the unfortunate effect of acting as a magnet to the Prince's political enemies. But often the Princess's amusements seem innocent enough: we read, for example, of two games of chess lost to Lord Minto, and of a discussion on the cultivation of flowers in a conservatory with Walter Scott. It is true that both Minto and Scott were alarmed by her flirtatious manner, and some of her guests certainly showed less restraint and discretion, but public opinion remained indulgent: sympathetic hearts warmed to a Princess left lonely and neglected by a selfish husband; and Caroline could count on a good reception by the people of London whenever she chose to go to town.

Sympathy with the Princess led to open abuse of the Prince, who was so conscious of his unpopularity that he spent much of 1796–7 away from the capital. The Light Dragoons were once more in camp at Brighton in midsummer of 1796 and the Prince visited them, his arrival coinciding with the first day of Brighton Races; but neither soldiering nor sport gave him much satisfaction that year. *The Times* had poured scorn on the social exclusiveness of Brighton Camp even before the Colonel-in-Chief reached his regiment; and its readers were led to believe that the camp motto was *'Vivent l'Amour et Bacchus'*. Everything the Prince wished to do was mocked in the Press. He retired to Dorset, renting Crichel House some five miles from Wimborne, although *The Times* – hotter in pursuit of the Prince than it was of Bonaparte – reported that he had taken no less than three houses at Bognor, and that a new London home was being created for Lady Jersey next to Carlton House. This constant hounding of the Prince, together with his own clumsy behaviour, led some members of the House of Commons to consider drawing up an Exclusion Bill, which would have denied the Prince any right of succession or power of regency; and, throughout 1797–8, the Tory newspapers would hint at the advisability of excluding him from the throne.

These were years of frustration and unhappiness for the Prince. He remained on terms of personal friendship with Fox and, for most of the time, with Sheridan, and he still reckoned himself to be, politically, a Foxite Whig; but some of the old 'Buff and Blues' had given him up as an insincere trifler, and among those who now distrusted him was Charles Grey. There was no doubt that the Prince's interests were changing, partly from personal quarrels and partly for reasons of economy. He no longer raced horses under his own colours; for there had been an unpleasant incident at Newmarket in October 1791 when a steward of the Jockey Club cast doubts on the honesty of one of his jockeys. More than thirty years were to elapse before the Prince was willing to appear again as the owner of runners at any meeting, although he enjoyed going to the races and placing heavy wagers. During these last years of the old century the Prince also seems momentarily to have lost his pleasure in music and he went far less to the theatre, probably from fear of how the audience would receive him. There were, of course, newer companions to amuse him, among them Captain George Brummell, who held a commission in the Prince's regiment for four years. Brummell's military career was distinguished by only three episodes: his inability on parade to remember which troop he commanded; his presence in the escort to Princess Caroline when she first arrived in England; and his abrupt resignation from the army on learning that the regiment was to be posted to Manchester. The Prince, however, enjoyed Brummell's company: he admired his technique for stiffening a cravat and the way in which he mixed his snuff; and much might be forgiven a fastidious arbiter of elegance with a sharp eye and a ready wit.

Yet, though he listened with awe to Brummell's strictures on sartorial taste, the Prince was under no illusions: he knew that Brummell's world was artificial and peopled with time-servers. Sometimes he grew weary of its empty folly. Once more he requested military promotion and fresh responsibilities, but his father still refused to take his soldiering seriously. In February 1797 the Prince showed a sudden interest in politics. He sent Pitt a long memorandum on the Irish Question in which he maintained that Ireland was menaced by an imminent French invasion and by Catholic rebellion. To ensure a continued British presence in Dublin the Prince proposed that all Catholic civil disabilities should be removed and that he himself should be entrusted 'to undertake the Government of Ireland, great and arduous as the task appears'. No response came from either the King or the Prime Minister: and the Prince of Wales was left to amuse himself, to calculate his debts, and to read the columns of abuse poured on him by an uninhibited Press. He continued to have hopes of excitement. One evening in February 1798, while he was still at Crichel, he sent an urgent message to the King informing him that an enemy fleet was reported to be off the Channel coast and that he was riding instantly to put himself at the head of his regiment, which was quartered in Dorchester barracks. Unfortunately, as the Duke of York explained patiently to him a few days later, the fleet 'was not an enemy but one of our own': and the Prince was again denied the chance to prove himself in battle. His dignified report commending the speed with which the Dorset Yeomanry had mobilised in Blandford did not entirely silence amusement in London; and it began to seem as if he was acquiring an unenviable genius for attracting ridicule. There were occasional flashes of Don Quixote's escapism in the Prince's character, and when the Light Dragoons were nearby his imagination tended to see the enemy in every windmill.

It was, however, his role as an ageing Don Juan that continued to titillate and amuse the gossips. The Countess of Jersey remained in close attendance on the Prince until the summer of 1798, when it became clear to everyone except herself that he was tired of her presence and looking elsewhere for companionship. Already he had amused himself briefly with Lady Horatia Seymour, a friend of Mrs Fitzherbert and a woman of spirit whom he had known long enough to quarrel with and to patch up old misunderstandings. He was, however, a trifle excessive in his mode of reconciliation; and in November Lady Horatia gave birth to a daughter, Mary ('Minnie'), for whom the Prince always felt deep affection, and with good reason.

His affair with Lady Horatia, whatever its consequences, was short-lived. He had long wished to resume his relationship with Mrs Fitzherbert, whom he continued to regard as the rightful 'wife of my heart and soul'; and he had sent his brother, Cumberland, to sound out her feelings as early as May 1796. But Mrs Fitzherbert, though willing to understand and excuse the dynastic marriage with Caroline, felt nothing but contempt for Lady Jersey and her circle. No more than the Princess was she prepared to share George's company with the Countess; and her conscience left her with genuine doubts over the morality of her own position. She would not hurry back to the Prince. Queen Charlotte wrote personally to her begging her to accept some new arrangement by which she could make the Prince happy; and he, for his part, continued to send her lockets and fresh pledges of love throughout the year 1799. At last she determined to seek the advice of her confessor and he duly appealed to Rome for guidance: was Mrs Fitzherbert wife to the Prince of Wales in the eyes of the Church or was she not? In May 1800, Pope Pius VII sent a message which reassured Maria Fitzherbert, though it showed discretion by avoiding canonical embarrassment: if the Prince 'was truly penitent for his sins and sincere in his promise of amendment' she 'might rejoin her husband'. The Prince was often penitent and always sincere, or so he believed; and Mrs Fitzherbert was satisfied. On 16 June she invited her London friends to a grand breakfast at her home in Tilney Street 'to meet His Royal Highness'.

Society, still unwilling to credit the secret marriage, was puzzled. She was rather stout and in her late forties, primly principled and unpretentiously domesticated. The Prince seemed to share nothing with her but an ample silhouette; and yet no one seeing them together at the theatre or on the Steine at Brighton could doubt their mutual contentment in those first six years of the new century. She mellowed his temper, and her own; she drastically cut his consumption of alcohol, although there were lapses now and again; and she imposed a tactful restraint on boisterous pursuits over-taxing to his constitution. Once he was reported seriously ill with 'inflammation of the stomach' and surgeons were summoned from London to Brighton to bleed him; but she nursed him back to health, keenly playing whist or loo with him in the evening and encouraging him to talk and mimic the politicians whom he encountered. Only a few friends perceived how much he needed her at this time.

While the Prince was rediscovering the comforts of life with Maria Fitzherbert, the Pitt administration ran into political difficulties and foundered. The troubled state of Ireland, aflame with insurrection, induced Pitt to propose a legislative union which would transfer the authority of the Irish Parliament in Dublin to Westminster; but he believed it essential to appease Irish indignation at this Act of Union by a measure of 'Catholic Emancipation', removing from the statute book all legislation which excluded Roman Catholics from Parliament and from executive office. The Prince of Wales had shown himself sympathetic to Catholic Emancipation, although it is likely that he retained considerable reservations over what should be done. George III, on the other hand, had no doubts over his course of action: he was convinced that Catholic Emancipation involved a breach of the oath he had taken at his coronation to govern and uphold the Church of England. The King's conscience was so troubled that he suffered a mental relapse and, for a fortnight in January 1801, all the old uncertainties and intrigues of the Regency Crisis came once more to the surface. But the King's illness was not so serious as in 1788 and by the end of the month his physicians were convinced he had recovered. He remained, however, obdurate: rather than remove Roman Catholic disabilities, he was prepared to dismiss the Prime Minister whose Government had held the nation together for seventeen years. On 14 March 1801, Henry Addington – a sensible mediocrity who had managed well enough as Speaker of the Commons for over a decade – surprised the country and himself by forming a Government; and Pitt was at last out of office.

The Prince of Wales took little part in this political crisis. He had never liked Pitt and was still sufficiently Foxite to be gratified by news of his fall; but he could feel no respect for Addington and distrusted his influence on the King. His hostility to Addington increased as the Government stumbled through the fourteen-month Peace of Amiens and into renewed war with France in May 1803. Invasion seemed again to threaten; and the Prince asked for a military command so as to set an example which would 'excite the loyal energies of the nation'. Addington ignored the request. On 2 August 1803 the Prince's Friends put forward his case in the House of Commons. Addington still equivocated. Four days later the Prince addressed an eloquent appeal to his father: 'I ask to be allowed to display the best energies of my character, to shed the last drop of my blood in support of your Majesty's person, crown and dignity.' The King appreciated the offer; privately he let his son know that he expected him to stand at his side in the field once the French invaders landed; but he refused to consider promotion or a command. There was some sympathy for the Prince: the Duke of York was a Field-Marshal and three of his other brothers were Lieutenant-Generals; but the heir to the throne remained a Colonel of Dragoons, a rank he had now held for ten years. At one moment George III became so irritated by his son's importunity that he even threatened to take this regiment away from him.

Unfortunately the Prince now made one of those indiscreet moves which so often placed him at a disadvantage. Shortly before Christmas he had all his correspondence over the military command published, so that the public might judge between father and son. But the dispute had dragged on too long and had become magnified; and the public was not particularly interested. The quarrel provided the satirists with a weapon and the Prince once again looked absurd. He merely succeeded in rousing his father's latent animosity; and for eleven months the King and the Prince avoided each other. In the spring of 1804 Pitt returned as Prime Minister; and the Prince continued to amuse himself with political intrigues that summer. He still regarded himself as a leader of the Whigs and, as the ebullient Creevey noted at the time, he loaded 'Fox with caresses'. And yet it is hard to say whether the Prince was acting from genuinely Whig sympathies or because he knew that the King had imposed a ban on Fox holding office when Pitt had sought to create a coalition. For the disappointment over his military command had brought out all the old pettiness in the Prince's attitude towards his father, and not even Mrs Fitzherbert could soothe his resentment.

Other problems pressed for solution. Princess Charlotte was growing up: by the autumn of 1804 she was a lively eight-year-old with a good ear for music and a stubborn temper. George III was convinced that the Prince of Wales could not be trusted to educate his granddaughter. He accordingly proposed that young Charlotte should come to Windsor where he intended that the Queen should bring her up in the family circle. At the same time he had every intention of ensuring that the child's mother saw far more of her daughter and he wrote to Princess Caroline at the end of November to let her know of his plans. The Prince, however, was furiously indignant and hastened to London. Yet for once good sense prevailed, largely thanks to the Queen. Early in the New Year it was agreed that Princess Charlotte would live in Carlton House (or in one of the adjoining houses in Pall Mall) so long as the Prince was in London, but when he was away from the capital her governesses would bring the child to Windsor or Kew. No one seemed willing to define what rights her mother would have.

This is hardly surprising. Strange rumours of what took place at Blackheath had been current in London for several years; and in the late autumn of 1805 such scandalous tales reached the ears of the Duke of Sussex that he urged his brother to take action. Lady Charlotte Douglas, a former neighbour of the Princess of Wales, testified that three years previously Caroline had taken her into her confidence and had admitted that she was mother of an infant boy, known as William Austin, who still slept in the Princess's room at Blackheath. The Prince of Wales was seriously alarmed by Lady Douglas's story. He let the King know that as 'a Father, a Husband and a Man of Honour' his feelings were wounded and, though it may have been difficult for George III to sympathise with his son in any of these capacities, he was quick to see that the child might one day challenge the succession; for Caroline had allegedly told Lady Douglas she would claim that the Prince was the boy's father, thereby excluding Princess Charlotte from the English throne and one of the King's sons from his dignities in Hanover. By now there was a coalition Government – 'the Ministry of All the Talents' – which was headed by Lord Grenville, for Pitt had died in January 1806. George III consulted Grenville and it was agreed to establish a Royal Commission which would examine all the allegations about the Princess of Wales and report back to the King. The Commissioners entrusted with this 'Delicate Investigation' were Grenville himself, the Lord Chancellor, the Lord Chief Justice and the Home Secretary.

They completed their work by midsummer. Caroline was cleared of the gravest charge, for the Commissioners were convinced that William Austin had been born into an impoverished labourer's family and informally adopted by the Princess as an act of charity. But they found her behaviour in other respects liable to 'very unfavourable interpretations'. She had romped familiarly with a number of naval officers: a servant had once fainted on accidentally seeing her immodest dallying with Admiral Sir Sidney Smith, though she did not limit her attentions to flag rank; and there was evidence that her conversation was frequently over-salted with sexual innuendo. George III was shocked by the report and by such of the testimony as was read to him, for he would not weary fading eyes by perusing it himself. He was principally offended by the numbers of men who had enjoyed Caroline's favours. Privately he declared that if 'it had been one attachment, and even a child, he would have screened her if he could have done it with safety to the Crown', but he could never condone profligacy on a scale of

45

such generosity. A royal reprimand was drafted, and it was intimated to the Princess of Wales that the King had no intention of receiving her at Court. Yet she did not entirely fall from grace. Within a year Spencer Perceval – a genuine friend to her and never her lover – became Chancellor of the Exchequer and he insisted on an outward reconciliation between the King and the Princess. Apartments were assigned to Caroline in Kensington Palace. Although she retained Blackheath as a residence, the naval officers of Greenwich found diversions less compromising to advancement in their sovereign's service, and for some years Caroline's own behaviour showed greater restraint.

The Delicate Investigation did not, as the Prince had hoped, provide him with such damning evidence of his wife's immorality that he could rid himself for all time of the 'fiend' from Brunswick. The whole episode lowered him still further in public regard. To many it seemed monstrous that, without a chance to speak in her own defence, his wife should be arraigned for lapses which appeared less grave than his own. The Prince was savagely mocked and lampooned, and he resented the attacks upon him, some of which showed a cruel lack of charity towards Mrs Fitzherbert. Moreover, during the very months of the Delicate Investigation, he had become a figure of major importance in the domestic politics of the country. When Pitt died, the Prince's Friends secured a large share of offices in the coalition ministry, and Fox himself became Leader of the Commons and Foreign Secretary. It was essential for the Whig members of the Government to consult the Prince over the thorny problem of Catholic Emancipation, which the King's apparent madness and the pusillanimity of Addington had left unresolved. Now that George III had controlled his prejudices sufficiently to make Fox a Secretary of State, it seemed reasonable to hope he might prove less intransigent over other matters. But the Prince knew his father's obstinacy. He told Fox that the Catholic Question had better be left alone so long as George III was alive; and he advised him to press the ministry for less factious measures of reform, such as abolition of the slave trade, rather than risk the furies aroused by any mention of Catholic relief.

Fox realised there was good sense in all the Prince said on this issue, and he did not raise the Catholic Question again. But, by midsummer 1806, it was beginning to look as if Fox were a dying man, for his legs were grossly swollen with dropsy. Through the dogdays of July and into

August he remained cooped up in his tiny house at Stable Yard, St James's Street, less than half a mile from Carlton House. The Prince visited him almost daily so long as he was in London and he held out the promise of recuperation at Brighton to his old friend. But early in September the Prince travelled up to Yorkshire and it was while he was at Wentworth House that he heard that Fox had died. He came south immediately, intending to pay final respects to his friend at the funeral in Westminster Abbey. The King, however, persisted in his belief that Fox was responsible for corrupting his son and he could not extend forgiveness to the Whig idol even in death: he curtly refused permission for the heir to the throne to participate in the ceremony at the Abbey, and the Prince was left to mourn Fox privately. No one doubted that he did so with sincerity, for he lost his appetite and began himself to look a sick man. Yet, if he resented the King's veto, he was also hurt by the failure of Grenville and Grey to discuss with him the future tactics of the Whigs. With Fox's death, the Prince drifted away from his old allies, and indeed from party politics. He insisted that his withdrawal came from his own choice, but some of his correspondence at the time suggests that it was prompted by pique at his treatment by Grenville (who headed the Conservative Whigs) and Grey (the leader of the more reformist faction in the party). Fox had known how to flatter the Prince by seeking advice: his heirs lacked his charm and his tact, and it was to cost the Whigs dearly.

The Prince remained in low spirits for several months after Fox's death, sitting strangely silent at dinner and sometimes with tears coursing down his flabby jowl. Gossip, which never gave him peace, said that he had fallen out with Mrs Fitzherbert and that he was infatuated with another grandmother, the Marchioness of Hertford, a terrifyingly haughty woman of nearly fifty who was matriarch of one of the staunchest Tory dynasties in the land. Curiously enough, he had come to know Lady Hertford principally because of Mrs Fitzherbert's desire to adopt Minnie Seymour, who had been left motherless before her third birthday. Minnie's mother, Horatia Seymour, made it clear in the year she died that she was willing to entrust the child to Maria Fitzherbert, but there was a long and involved legal dispute with the Seymour family (of whom Lord Hertford was a member) who objected to Minnie being brought up by a Roman Catholic. The whole affair received astonishing publicity, which culminated in a savage satirical print by Gillray full of extreme Protestant prejudice. But eventually in June 1806 the Hertfords agreed to allow Mrs Fitzherbert to act as Minnie's guardian, as the child herself wished. The Prince threw a children's party at the Pavilion to celebrate the happy outcome of the dispute; and for the moment it looked as if the rumour-mongers would be confounded. But he could not shake off his desire for Lady Hertford's company, and poor Maria Fitzherbert saw far less of him that winter.

So, indeed, did everyone else. Discretion had hurried the Marchioness of Hertford off to her estates in Ireland and the Prince appears to have found the days long and tedious. He designed a new uniform for the Tenth Hussars (ex-Light Dragoons), a regiment which had survived thirteen years of war without sighting an enemy or any shore more foreign than the Isle of Wight. The officers looked magnificent in yellow boots, red breeches and a lace-encrusted jacket; and only the more exclusive women of the town modelled their fashions on the Prince's Own Hussars. But London seemed dead to him and Brighton cold. In the following August, however, he celebrated his forty-fifth birthday with characteristic panache at his Pavilion by the sea. It was a grand occasion: a mock encounter between ships at sea; a review on the Downs; the Prince in a diamond-studded colonel's uniform, massive on a grey charger; bands playing on the lawns; dancing and refreshment in the afternoon; fireworks and a banquet in the evening. Five royal dukes were among the guests and Princess Charlotte, wearing a white muslin dress and a gypsy hat trimmed with roses, was driven over from Worthing in an open barouche with her governess. Everyone, it seemed, had come that Wednesday to congratulate the Prince; and the scene stands vivid in the pages of reminiscence as if caught in a pictorial album. Yet there is someone missing from the picture. Minnie Seymour was present, but not her guardian. They said Mrs Fitzherbert was indisposed. A few days later the Prince set out for Cheltenham; and malicious pens noted that it was within a carriage drive of Ragley Hall, Hertford's seat on the borders of Warwickshire and Worcestershire.

The shadows fell on Maria Fitzherbert's house at the corner of the Steine. She remained devoted to the Prince for the rest of his life but she was never prepared to share his favours with any mistress. Although he continued to refer to her in his letters as 'dearest Mrs Fitzherbert', they were little closer than mere acquaintances when the Regency began in 1811. Should the Prince wish to return to her for a second time, she was willing to rekindle their domestic happiness. Meanwhile, she lived out her life free from vindictiveness or resentment: she had an allowance of £6,000 a year, the companionship of an adopted daughter, and above all she had social standing and dignity. Far better to be treated with a queenly deference in Brighton than jostled by social climbers at Carlton House. A strange marriage passed into a strange separation.

4

The Coming of the Regency 1807–14

On 15 August 1807, the Saturday following the Prince's festivities in Brighton, another birthday was celebrated across the Channel. In the Palace of St Cloud the Emperor Napoleon received the congratulations of his marshals and ministers on attaining the age of thirty-eight. The contrast between these two occasions, separated by only three days in time but by an epoch in history, was significant. The heir of England, Scotland, Ireland and Hanover played at soldiering in the mimic world of his own creation: the ruler of the French, newly-returned to Paris with victories from the East, basked in the splendours of a borrowed ceremonial. While the Prince of Wales at forty-five was still denied power of responsibility, Napoleon had reached the apogee of his amazing career. He held, he thought, all Europe in the palm of his hand. That day French troops were parading in Antwerp and Bremen and Warsaw, French bugles sounded out across the lagoon at Venice and echoed around the foothills of the Pyrenees; and at night French camp fires glowed in the sky along Dutch and German coasts, above the Rhine and the Inn, and down the long line of the Tyrrhenian shore. Only the British continued to defy Napoleon's authority. In the gale-tossed waters of Biscay and in calmer southern seas three-deckers and frigates kept his captains conscious of naval power and of the enduring victory won at Trafalgar two years before. But Napoleon himself did not rate highly the challenge from beyond the Channel, nor anticipate that it would be long maintained. Already the Continental System had closed most European ports to British trade; and he was convinced that the commercial classes would soon turn against a war which denied them markets. Moreover he did not believe the English people would readily steel themselves to accept the privations of counter-blockade. Except for the fourteen months of armed truce in 1802–3, the British had been at war for almost a decade and a half, a longer period of belligerency than in any conflict since Elizabethan times. With Russia now allying herself with France, it seemed unlikely that a general peace would be long delayed.

In London there was indeed no sign of sustained military resolution. Apart from some sharp actions in southern Italy, British troops had not participated in serious operations against the French for some twelve years; and, since the deaths of Pitt and Fox, no man of stature had emerged to give purpose to the nation's feats of arms. Political faction ludicrously mocked the apparent intentions of government. The Whig leaders, divided from each other and from the King, resigned office in March 1807 rather than give George III a written undertaking never to seek from him concessions for Roman Catholics in the higher com-mands of the army. They were succeeded by a Tory administration, nominally headed by the Duke of Portland, but once again without any clear direction. For two years the country stumbled forward: energetic action at Copenhagen prevented the Danish fleet passing into French hands; an expeditionary force, hurriedly improvised in Ireland, found itself encouraging a Spanish revolt against French domination; but a more ambitious enterprise against the Dutch island of Walcheren ended in disaster. The Government looked shabbier than ever: two of its youngest and ablest members – Castlereagh and Canning – quarrelled so bitterly that they fought a duel on Putney Heath and excluded themselves momentarily from office. Portland died at the end of 1809 and was succeeded as Prime Minister by Spencer Perceval. It seemed to make little difference. Cheap coloured prints reproduced the ferocious caricatures of George Cruikshank and James Gillray, radicals who ridiculed the pretentious at home and abroad. Nor was popular criti-cism limited to visual cartoons. The satirical sheets and pamphlets of William Hone and Thomas Wooler provided a violent commentary on the incompetence of the Tory Government. Few people wanted peace without victory, for there was an instinctive English patriotism which Napoleon was never able to comprehend; but many began to despair of seeing the war brought to a successful end so long as such an inept administration remained at the head of affairs.

Inevitably some of this withering public contempt was turned against the Prince of Wales and his brothers, all of whom possessed a strange ability to blunder foolishly in personal relations, and most of whom showed an absence of restraint in money matters. The Prince himself was probably the best of the brood and certainly the most intelligent. The Duke of Clarence (the future William IV) lived in happy poverty with the actress Mrs Jordan and their ten children: he was content to play the part of a retired seadog, swearing thunderous obscenities and yet remaining heartily affable; and, had he come from a less vulgar family, he might well have figured as a character in one of Jane Austen's novels. By contrast, the Duke of Kent was universally detested, having been retired from the army in 1803 after his brutality had provoked a mutiny at Gibraltar; and the Duke of Cumberland, who never hid his reactionary politics, was commonly believed to be an incestuous pervert of alarming temper. The eccentricities of George III's sixth and seventh surviving sons, the Dukes of Sussex and Cambridge, were harmlessly mild, and Cambridge even had an endearing habit of heckling preachers who inserted rhetorical questions in their sermons; but neither man was likely to strengthen the dignity of the Crown by his personality. The old King's favourite son remained the Duke of York, his second child; but in 1809 the Duke was disgraced when it was revealed in the House of Commons that his mistress, Mary Anne Clarke, had made a pretty profit by acting as broker in the sale of military commissions and promotions. It was even alleged that the Duke of York, who was always short of funds, had taken a share of the proceeds; and for two months the House examined a succession of dubious witnesses before clearing his name of corruption or of connivance at corruption. But the Duke had allowed Mrs Clarke so much interference in official business that it was thought better for him to resign as Commander-in-Chief of the army. Both Cruikshank and Gillray sharpened their pens on the Duke's fallen reputation.

George III was distressed by the Mary Anne Clarke scandal and he was soon saddened still more by the illness of his youngest daughter, Princess Amelia, of whom he was especially fond. She died from consumption early in November 1810. A few days later the King's attendants noticed that he was beginning to let his talk ramble on inconsequentially when he was out riding; and by the end of the month he was once more suffering from delusions, the slim thread of reason shattered by his favourite son's disgrace and his favourite daughter's death. Reassuring bulletins were issued throughout the first half of December but Spencer Perceval was shrewd enough to suspect undue optimism among the King's physicians and on 15 December he appointed a Committee of Peers to enquire into the sovereign's mental condition. There seemed a good prospect that he would recover his faculties within a few weeks, but on the last day of 1810 Spencer Perceval introduced a Regency Bill into the Commons. It was based on Pitt's proposals of twenty-two years previously, including the imposition of restraints for twelve months upon the Regent's prerogatives.

The Prince of Wales was understandably irritated. In 1788 he had been a comparatively young man: now he was nearly fifty and it was humiliating to be told by Parliament that for a year he could take no measures of a lasting character. He summoned his brothers to Carlton House and they signed a joint letter to the Prime Minister protesting at limitations which, they claimed, ran counter to 'principles which seated our family upon the throne of these realms'. The Prince also sent for the Whig leaders, Grey and Grenville, though it was clear they did not share his views on every question. The Whig rank and file were in high spirits, playing once more the delightful game of Cabinet-making: no one nowadays rated Sheridan's chances of the Exchequer highly, but that enlightened brewer, Samuel Whitbread, dined out several nights on the prospects of the Foreign Office and of a negotiated peace with the French. Young Lord Palmerston, at twenty-six a Tory and Secretary at War, jauntily observed 'We are all for the kick and go'; but he was wrong. The Prince, though making it clear he had no confidence in Perceval's administration, let it be publicly known that he would not change the government so long as it seemed likely that George III's sanity would be restored. On 5 February 1811 the Prince was duly sworn in as Regent of the United Kingdom at a Privy Council in Carlton House. Lest any doubt might linger of the Prince's traditional allegiance, Tory ministers arriving for the Council found themselves confronted by a massive bust of Charles James Fox. Outside a regimental band played 'God Save the King' several times over. It was, at that moment, a prayer dear to every Tory heart.

There seemed no reason why the Regent should lose his antipathy towards Perceval, who had befriended Princess Caroline, and the Whigs remained confident of office when the 'probationary' year expired, and even sooner if George III died during the summer, as many expected.

54

And yet, as the Prince of Wales became accustomed to the pleasures of authority, doubts began to trouble some back-benchers. They found him pompously remote, strangely silent at Carlton House receptions. Gossip, as usual, blamed everything on that arch-Tory harridan Lady Hertford, but careful observation could find nothing more sinister to report than that the Prince and the Marchioness were 'supposed to be engaged with religion and read daily a chapter or two of the Bible'. Mr Creevey, Whig member for Thetford and liveliest of the classic letter-writers, was not wholly convinced the Prince remained a sincere Foxite. On the third Saturday in July he dashed an indignant note off to his wife informing her that he had passed the windows of the Prime Minister's kitchen and there observed 'four man cooks and twice as many maids preparing dinner for the Prince of Wales'. If the Regent was supping with Perceval, then old affronts were forgotten and past loyalties counted little. 'By God!' wrote Creevey. 'This is too much.'

All through the autumn the Whigs anxiously interpreted the Regent's gestures and silences and table-talk. He seemed highly critical of Viscount Wellington's operations in Portugal; and this was seen as a good sign, for Wellington's brother, the Marquess of Wellesley, was Foreign Secretary and a possible contender for the Tory succession. The Regent's actions were more puzzling than his conversation. For the Colonel of the Tenth Hussars to make himself a Field-Marshal was understandable if precipitate, but it was positively disconcerting to find him reinstating the Duke of York as Commander-in-Chief less than two years after his disgrace. Creevey, sharing the disapproval of most back-benchers, hurried up to Westminster from Brighton to vote against the Duke's reappointment. Yet moral indignation was easily stilled. The Brighton Season was at its height and in the following fortnight Creevey accepted the Regent's hospitality in the Royal Pavilion on six evenings, meticulously noting the triviality of pleasure in his journal. We see Prinny 'very fat . . . in his full Field Marshal's uniform' happily watching his footmen taking round iced champagne punch, lemonade and sandwiches at midnight, or on other evenings in the Music Room, sometimes 'actually singing and very loud too' and sometimes content to thump a massive royal thigh in time to the band. He was in boisterous spirits that winter, though early in December his enthusiasm ran away with him; for having determined to show Princess Charlotte how a Highland fling should be done, he came down

so heavily on his ankle that he was forced to retire to bed for a fortnight, groaning in agony and heavily dosed with laudanum. A tactless
remark by his brother Cumberland that what the Regent wanted was a
poultice on the head rather than on the ankle imposed a strain on the
Christmas festivities; for, in this particular family, such comments were
in distinctly poor taste.

The Regent had recovered by the New Year and was ready to face a
major political crisis; for he had resolved to make no change in the
leadership of the Government. This was a wise decision: the war at
last was going well along the Portuguese and Spanish frontier, where
Wellington's men stormed Ciudad Rodrigo deep in January snow and
prepared to move against Salamanca and Badajoz in the south. The
Peninsular War, on which the Regent had so recently poured scorn, now
captured his imagination; and Wellington was encouraged, as soon as
the Regent had the power to create peerages, by an earldom and by an
annuity of £2,000 voted by a grateful Parliament. It seemed to the
Regent out of the question to entrust government to men who were
lukewarm in support of the campaign. He informed Grey and Grenville
that he was determined to keep Perceval in office, but he invited the
Whigs to accept posts in the administration so as to form a broad-based
coalition. Grey, however, and most of his supporters, wanted a negotiated peace; and Grenville openly favoured the return of all British
troops from the Iberian Peninsula. Moreover, the Whigs still sought an
assurance of political emancipation for the Roman Catholics; and this
pledge the Regent, despite his earlier sympathy with the Foxites, was
not now prepared to give. The Whigs accordingly remained in Opposition, though the Duke of Northumberland in the Lords and the numeri-
cally small Sheridan faction in the Commons gave their support to the
Regent. But most of the Whigs regarded the Prince's decision as
treachery. They never forgave him for what they felt to be a betrayal
of Fox's hallowed memory, though it is reasonable to suppose that had
Fox survived he would hardly have condemned his party to such rigid
attachment to principles.

While there was still a prospect of obtaining office when the Prince
of Wales came into his own, the Whigs had been prepared to look
benevolently on his folly. Even so late as June 1811, when he held a
grand fête at Carlton House for the exiled Bourbons of France, they

gratefully accepted his hospitality, delighting in the two-hundred-foot-long supper table, in the artificial stream which flowed between banks of flowers through the Gothic Conservatory, and the endless dishes of food 'in and out of season' with which two thousand guests were fortified in the small hours of the morning. A radical poet like Shelley might condemn such extravagance, 'a bauble . . . to amuse this over-grown bantling of Regency'; but no Whig voices were raised in protest. A year later it was different. Even such a restrained and responsible statesman as Grey could warn his brother peers of 'an influence of odious character' which 'lurked behind the throne', although they might be excused for failing to recognise in this unlikely guise the Marquess of Hertford's consort. Less balanced figures allowed frustration to swing their emotions more strongly against the Prince. Henry Brougham, a brilliant advocate, and Samuel Whitbread, a mis-placed idealist, championed the wrongs of the Princess of Wales with all the zeal they had shown on worthier causes of reform. With some relish, Brougham let it be known he intended to denounce the Regent 'in terms which would not have been too strong to have described the later days of Tiberius'; and when, in March 1812, Sheridan declared at a freemasons' dinner that he would willingly lay down his life for the Prince's principles, his magnanimous offer was received with long and sustained hisses rather than with the silent incredulity it deserved.

There was, of course, a good case which any Opposition could make against the Regent and against Perceval's government of the country. But the Whigs, like the radical press and the angry young poets, con-centrated too much on personalities and not enough on policies. Out-side London and the comfortable towns of southern England, morale reached a lower point in the winter of 1811–12 than at any other moment during the Napoleonic Wars. The industrialism of recent decades, which for long had promised prosperity, now threw up prob-lems of uncertainty. The months in which the Whigs were charging the Regent with apostasy witnessed a grimmer mood of disillusionment in the Midlands and in Lancashire and Cheshire, where angry mobs smashed machines in desperate revulsion at their changed way of life. Food was everywhere scarce and expensive, with wheat costing three times its pre-war price; and the lack of export markets was hitting the great textile centres, filling the new towns of Lancashire and Yorkshire with unemployment. During August 1810, almost unnoticed in London, five firms in Manchester went into liquidation, sending shock waves of bankruptcy across the northern counties for the following eighteen months. This was a harsh world for the Regent and his friends, as far removed from fashionable Regency dandyism as from the agrarian economy of an earlier age. It was also a hidden world – at least until 11 May 1812. For on that Monday afternoon, shortly after five o'clock, a bankrupt commercial agent named John Bellingham brought the burdens of his troubled mind into the margin of history by assassinating Spencer Perceval in the lobby of the House of Commons. Next morning an anonymous letter arrived at Carlton House addressed to the Prince's Secretary and signed 'Vox Populi' which threatened the Regent with Perceval's fate unless the price of bread was speedily reduced; and at Nottingham there was such rejoicing in the streets at the news of Perceval's murder that troops were called out and the Riot Act read by the local magistrates. In many parts of the country there was an ugly mood that spring.

The Prince Regent behaved admirably in this unexpected crisis. He refused to take panic measures or to let the recent bitterness of the Whigs blind him to their merits. For almost two months he conducted negotiations with each of the political factions, striving once more to create that broad patriotic coalition which he believed would win the war speedily and thus ease the trade slump imposed by the closure of Europe's markets. He would have liked the Government to be headed by Wellesley, but he again found that the suspicions which separated Tories from Whigs (and, in some instances, Tories from Tories) were too great for a comprehensive administration. Early in June, he turned as a compromise candidate to the Earl of Liverpool. Nobody could say he had any rare qualities of mind, nor did he show powers of leadership; but he was a skilled debater with an unruffled temperament and he had always made a capable chairman of committees. When Creevey heard that the Regent had invited Liverpool to form a government he wrote bluntly in his journal, 'Well, this is beyond anything!'; and there were many at Westminster who agreed with him. Yet Liverpool proved himself able to hold together Cabinets containing strong (and often conflicting) personalities. Rather surprisingly, he remained Prime Minister for nearly fifteen years, a period of continuous office longer than those of any of his successors and one which was exceeded among his predecessors only by Walpole and Pitt. The Liverpool Ministry had little to offer the rapidly growing population of the country in home affairs: it never solved the conflict of labourers and manufacturers, and it sought to strengthen authority in the troubled areas of the North and the Midlands by imposing ferocious penalties, cowing the workers by threats of hanging or transportation. But in foreign affairs the administration, backed by Wellington's victories, achieved a success denied to any British Government for more than half a century. The Regent gained a prestige in Europe which almost measured up to the high estimate he had made of his own stature.

Although politics and war increasingly cast their fascination on the Prince, he still liked to think of himself as a patron of the arts. When he attended the annual banquets of the Royal Academy, he always gave special attention to his speech and was heard with respect as an authority on collections of paintings and furniture. He genuinely wished to encourage pride in artistic achievement as a national characteristic and tried to combat the mildly philistine taste of the English aristocracy, though it must be admitted that his own aesthetic sense had a personal quality not everyone could appreciate. It would appear that he was a sound judge of seventeenth-century Dutch painting and he had a good eye for the beauty of French furniture and English china; but as a builder and decorator – and, indeed, as a collector of silver – he seems to have found it difficult to curb that instinct for almost vulgar ostentation which invariably found free rein in his sense of dress and costume. He was assisted, in the early days of the Regency, by the good advice of Lord Hertford and by the genius of John Nash, an architect who had first attracted his attention as early as 1798, but whose greatest years of achievement coincided with the peak of the Regency decade.

There was a long and sympathetic partnership between Nash and the Prince. The best-known example of their co-operation is the Oriental extravaganza at Brighton, where, between 1815 and 1820, Nash rebuilt the Pavilion. But their most ambitious project was in the capital itself; for, in 1811, the Regent discussed with Nash a plan which would give the West End of London an impressive and orderly system of streets, squares and open places. Nash proposed the construction of a line of elegant buildings which would stretch for over two miles southwards from the picturesquely formal Regent's Canal around the gardens, lawns and villas of a new park to a crescented colonnade east of St Marylebone

Church; and he then envisaged a 'Royal Mile' of stucco terraces from Portland Place down the magnificent pivotal panorama of Regent Street to end in a final flourish of Ionic columns at the approach to Carlton House. The original design, which Nash published in 1812, was more ambitious than anything he executed in the twenty years which he devoted to reshaping London. He saw Regent's Park, for example, as a succession of wooded groves separating clusters of villas from a grand double circus surrounding a pleasure pavilion similar to the *Lusthaus* which the Emperor Joseph II had erected in the Vienna Prater; but only eight villas were constructed in Regent's Park, and much of Nash's vision remained fantasy in a sketch-book. Yet, even in its truncated form, the project is the most dramatic attempt made by any English architect to create a sense of space and symmetry within the capital city. It urbanised the characteristically eighteenth-century feeling for landscape and, though the details of Nash's work may have been French in inspiration, it retained the self-assured naturalness of the English country houses. None of this project could have been achieved without the patronage and encouragement of the Prince whose name and dignity it so frequently commemorated; for ultimately it was the Regent's authority which enabled Nash to cut through the legal tangles of the Crown Commissioners and to confound the timidity of men less lavish in their style. Only Charles II among English sovereigns enriched the heritage of London as much as the Prince of Wales in his years of Regency.

He was never such a close patron of literature, but no person of cultured breeding could ignore the impulse given to creative writing by poets and novelists as they searched for new ways of expression. Wordsworth, Keats, Shelley and Byron wrote their major works during the Regency. The Prince, though a Romantic in his desire not to be confined by artistic convention, was too concerned with stability of government to appreciate the radical poets; but in the summer of 1812 he did at least hold a remarkable conversation with Byron, who was a guest at a ball graced by the Regent's presence. Though much of their talk was concerned with the virtues of Walter Scott, Byron was impressed by the Regent's critical taste and gratified by 'sayings peculiarly pleasing from royal lips' which praised his own work; he even amused himself by the thought that one day he might be Poet Laureate. Scott's verses were much more to the Regent's taste and he always made a considerable fuss of 'dear Walter', who purred contentedly at every mark of encouragement. The Regent is also reported to have enjoyed the novels of Jane Austen. When she was in London in the autumn of 1815 she was told that he kept a set of her works at each of the royal residences. Subsequently she was invited to visit Carlton House and was shown around the library by one of the Regent's domestic chaplains. Although Jane Austen had always sympathised with Princess Caroline rather than with her husband, she was so flattered by tales of princely favour that she sought permission to dedicate her newest novel, *Emma*, to His Royal Highness. His chaplain wrote to her in March 1816, letting her know that the Prince was pleased by the dedication and by the specially-bound edition sent to him by her publishers, but the Regent does not appear to have left any written comments on her novels, nor did they exchange direct correspondence. It is a pity they did not meet, for it would have been interesting to see what impression a prose caricaturist of such gently barbed skill received of the man the lampoonists so savagely derided in their political cartoons.

While the Prince Regent – and much of the English nobility with him – was enjoying *Sense and Sensibility* and *Pride and Prejudice*, the long foreign war at last reached its climax. On the same night that the Regent had his one conversation with Byron, the Emperor Napoleon followed the Grand Army across the River Niemen and down the long road towards Vilna, Smolensk and Moscow. Soon half a million men were moving relentlessly eastwards through the midsummer heat. British hopes in July and August 1812 rested not with the Russians, for whose constancy in war most people in London had little respect as yet, but with Wellington's men in the Peninsula, as they moved forward through Salamanca to Madrid until the autumn rains caught them beneath the fortress guns of Burgos. But, by the end of November, rumours began to seep through to England of a French disaster in Russia and *The Times* printed reports of Napoleon's death in the snows. Though the Emperor survived the campaign, it was clear that France could not now win the war; and in the following year new victories and new allies finally tipped the scale against Napoleon. Spain was cleared and, for the first time, British regiments (including the Tenth Hussars) stood on the line of the Pyrenees; while, as winter came once more, a broken French army fell back across Germany from Leipzig to the Rhine. In the opening weeks of 1814, amid colder weather than anyone in western Europe could remember, the Russians, Prussians and Austrians penetrated slowly southwestwards towards Paris as Wellington advanced on Toulouse. At the end of March the Tsar of Russia and the King of Prussia rode into Paris, while Castlereagh (who, as Foreign Secretary, represented the Regent in the supreme counsels of the Allies) remained with the Austrians in Dijon. On 6 April Napoleon signed an act of abdication; and peace broke out.

For most of these exciting months we catch only occasional glimpses of the Regent, still moving round from Carlton House to Brighton and Windsor and up to York. There was a dramatic incident, at the end of July 1813, which brought muted echoes of a frivolous past. A select 'Dandy Ball' was given by Lord Alvanley at the Argyle Rooms, at which the Regent was the guest of honour. But also present was Beau Brummell, long under a cloud of displeasure for slights to Maria Fitzherbert. The Regent, seeing Brummell as soon as he arrived, cut him dead; and Brummell, knowing how to wound the Prince's self-esteem, enquired loudly, 'Alvanley, who's your fat friend?' It was an impertinence which the Regent, though generous by nature, could never forgive. Brummell's eclipse was now as inevitable as Bonaparte's.

The Prince, however, wasted little time over such trivialities that summer. He was genuinely interested in grand strategy and the problems of diplomacy which accompanied it. Unlike his brothers, he was able to keep in his head the complicated details of negotiation. He identified himself closely with the changing fortunes of war, never hesitating to claim credit when he thought it merited. At times it must be admitted that his reasoning is hard to follow. Thus, on 6 December 1812, he wrote to Queen Charlotte, about 'the great and glorious news from Russia of which I have, under Providence, the heartfelt consolation, without unbecoming vanity, to ascribe in a great degree to my own original and indefatigable endeavours in drawing that Power to those measures which have since been pursued'; and after Leipzig he even sent his mother a snuffbox bearing his portrait as 'one I hope you will think is no disgrace to you'. No doubt he felt himself present in spirit at the conference which preceded the pursuit of Napoleon to the Beresina and at 'the battle of the Nations'; but there are moments when the borderline between reality and illusion seems to have become pathetically blurred in his mind.

The most moving of his letters was sent at the news of the fall of Paris in April 1814. Writing, as he said, 'in a very trembling and hardly intelligible hand', he declared to the Queen, 'I trust my dearest mother that you will think I have fulfilled and done my duty at least, and perhaps I may be vain enough to hope that you feel a little proud of your son'. It was more than twenty-one years since he had accompanied the first British contingent as it left London for the wars. To his regret he had never once seen action or even set foot outside England. And yet was it really preposterous of him to seek a share in the triumph of the hour? He had kept from office those who wished for a compromise peace in 1811 and he had given his confidence to Wellington's army in the Peninsula when the dusty hills of Portugal seemed terribly distant from Paris. The Emperors of Austria and Russia and the King of Prussia may, in the end, have ridden against Napoleon; but they had also ridden beside him. The Prince Regent's record was, at all events, consistent: he deserved some sprigs of the laurel wreath.

1 George as Prince of Wales, dressed in the uniform of the Royal Kentish Bowmen and leaning on a statue of Diana. Painting by Russell

II and III Mrs Fitzherbert, the Prince's morganatic wife: *above* as depicted by Thomas Gainsborough; *below* a less kindly representation – a cartoon from *Fashionable Follies*, 1802, showing her awaiting the Prince

iv   Caroline of Brunswick, by Sir Thomas Lawrence

v In 1811 George eventually was made Prince Regent, and this
cartoon mocks the new Regent with his corsets and his perfumes

VI and VII. Two of John Nash's designs for the Royal Pavilion at Brighton: *above*, the exterior; *below*, the Banqueting Room

The COURT at Brighton à la Chinese !!

Gent   no Gent   & Re gent !!

VIII One member of Parliament described the Regent's Court at the Pavilion as resembling more 'the pomp and magnificence of a Persian satrap in all the splendour of Oriental state than the sober dignity of a British prince . . .'. Cruikshank took a similar view, as shown in his cartoon of the 'Court at Brighton à la Chinese', 1816

IX Cruikshank's satirical comment upon the Regency, from a cartoon of 1816. Once more the Oriental style of Brighton Pavilion is caricatured in the right-hand part of the cartoon

x   The coronation banquet of George IV, a painting by Jones. The banquet took place on 19 July 1821 in Westminster Hall. The King sits in the centre surrounded by his brothers and his son-in-law, Prince Leopold. Before them stands the King's Champion, attended by the Lord High Constable and the Deputy Earl Marshal

XI 'Baise-mon', a cartoon of 1820, showing the King with his last mistress, Lady Conyngham

5

Contrasts of Victory 1814–15

In later years people remembered 1814 as 'the year of revelry', and with good reason. Strictly speaking, the festivities began in London many weeks before final victory in Europe: it was such a cold winter that the Thames froze solid from Blackfriars to London Bridge, and no one could resist the attractions of a Frost Fair on the ice. But the real rejoicing did not start until the second week of April, when messages from Paris confirmed the news that Napoleon had abdicated. The capital was illuminated for three successive nights; and so, in a sense, were many of its citizens. All classes of society sought to show their relief that the long wars had at last ended. The Prince Regent, in residence at a much be-flagged Carlton House, was genuinely proud to symbolise a Britain triumphant. By nature a supreme major-domo, he was determined to celebrate the coming of peace in appropriate style. He would honour Louis XVIII, about to return to Paris after exiled years of gout and obscurity, and he would invite the Allied rulers and generals to cross from France, so as to share with him the pleasures of victory. In this happiest of spring-times there seemed every reason to hope that the Prince's sense of occasion, which never failed to impress loyal friends in Brighton, would carry him majestically through parades, galas and banquets until dignity and charm silenced the critics at home and won him respect from his brother sovereigns.

The celebrations began well enough. On 20 April Louis XVIII emerged from his Buckinghamshire sanctuary at Hartwell and passed through cheering crowds in Aylesbury and Tring and Berkhamsted to Stanmore, where the Regent greeted him warmly. At three in the afternoon a procession of seven carriages, escorted by a troop of Life Guards, duly trundled off from Stanmore down the Edgware Road and made a State Entry into Piccadilly. King Louis stayed for three nights at Grillon's

Hotel in Albemarle Street, where there was a happy exchange of orders of chivalry, the Prince Regent stooping low to buckle the Garter around a knee grosser even than his own. More cheers rang out next day as Louis drove to Carlton House for a splendid dinner. *The Times* declared, somewhat grandly, that both the Regent of England and the King of France had done their duty and 'have merited and have obtained the applause of Mankind'. Then on 23 April, King Louis set off for Dover, escorted by the Dukes of Kent and Sussex, while the Prince Regent himself went ahead to ensure that every honour would be observed at the port of embarkation. As the royal yacht sailed out towards Calais, the Regent led the cheering for the new master of France, bowing with dignity as the vessel reached the pierhead. It is a pity Louis did not witness these attentions: he was in his cabin, so fortified against the indignities of a crossing that he was already fast asleep. Fortunately a royal member of his entourage possessed sufficient courage to face the waters of the harbour; and the Regent, who does not seem to have perceived any shrinkage in the figure on deck, returned to London gratified that courtesies had been fulfilled and acknowledged. The prospects looked good for the State Visit of the Tsar of Russia and the King of Prussia in June. The Emperor of Austria had also been invited, but he declined to make the journey because he hated public occasions and was anxious to return to Vienna. He accordingly sent the Austrian Foreign Minister, Prince Metternich, as his personal representative; and the two monarchs and Metternich crossed to Dover on 6 June.

The State Visit was far more pleasing for the Regent in anticipation than in fulfilment. Inevitably the people of London paid tribute to the heroes of the day rather than to the master of ceremonies. They cheered Blücher, the Prussian commander; they cheered Platov, the leader of the Russian Cossacks; and, if they showed only scant interest in Frederick William III of Prussia and in Metternich, they remained fascinated by Tsar Alexander I. Already that spring there had been a brisk trade in pamphlets which praised his virtues: he was 'the Christian Conqueror' in one; and 'the Saviour of Paris' in another. Though in reality the Tsar took little part in the harassment of Napoleon until the autumn of 1813, he was popularly identified with the Russian people's heroic defiance of the French invaders in 1812, and he was fêted accordingly. For three weeks the English Press, whether radical or respectable, recorded his progress with reverential awe.

Every minor detail was carefully reported, from the first arrival at Pulteney's Hotel in Piccadilly until his final departure for Ostend and ultimately for St Petersburg. His visits to the theatre and to Covent Garden, to Westminster and Greenwich and Oxford, his day at Ascot Races, his moments of religious devotion with the Quakers or in a Russian Orthodox Chapel – nothing was omitted. No member of the British Royal Family – and certainly never the Prince of Wales – had received such unctuous treatment from the newspapers.

The Prince Regent was soon in the lowest of spirits. He had hoped to bask momentarily in the reflected glory of victory: he found instead that his image was distorted, as though by some mocking mirror. On the very afternoon of the Tsar's welcome to Piccadilly, the Prince was advised not to appear in the streets of London for fear of hostile demonstrations by supporters of Princess Caroline. The Regent received little honour or recognition from his guests, and virtually none from the English people. Only Metternich, whom he had first met in London twenty years previously, pleased him. He was delighted to become the first Protestant Prince to be given the Order of the Golden Fleece, and he was childishly happy with the honorary colonelcy of a Hungarian regiment, for the uniform corresponded closely with his own extravagant mode of dress. Metternich, he thought, was the 'wisest of ministers'; and this partiality towards the Austrian statesman certainly had some influence on British attitudes during the peace-making of the following fifteen months. Far more important, however, was the negative fact that the Prince Regent came to dislike Tsar Alexander intensely. The two men, though outwardly so different in character, were both romantic escapists, given at times to exhibitionism. But the Tsar had actually ridden into Paris as a conqueror, the first foreign prince to do so since Henry v of England four centuries previously. Even without the English Press, it is unlikely that the Prince Regent would have warmed to the Tsar's personality. Alexander, for his part, made no effort to hide his contempt for his host; and his public and private remarks shocked both the Tory Government and the Whig Opposition. Socially there is no doubt that the Tsar's visit was a disaster.

The fault was not entirely Alexander's. He had been preceded to London by his sister, the Grand-Duchess Catherine, who staggered society by her monumental bad manners and lack of political sense. At a formal dinner in Carlton House she appalled the Prince Regent by asking for the band to be sent away, since the sound of music always produced in her a sensation of nausea; and she then proceeded to lecture the Prince on the best way of introducing Princess Charlotte into society and on the happy relations which, she insisted, should always exist between a husband and his wife. Only a threat of immediate resignation from an exasperated Russian ambassador dissuaded her from paying a formal call on the Princess of Wales. The Grand Duchess escorted her brother the Tsar throughout the State Visit; and demanded she should accompany him to the Guildhall Banquet on 18 June, where the Corporation of the City of London entertained seven hundred guests to a dinner which was, according to the *Annual Register*, 'as sumptuous as expense or skill could make it'. On this occasion the Grand Duchess asked the Lord Mayor to omit the singing of patriotic songs by artists from the Italian Opera, though her digestion permitted the playing of the National Anthem after the royal toast. The Tsar distinguished himself by halting suddenly as the procession moved up to the dais in order to exchange a few words with Lord Grey, thereby arresting the Prince Regent's stately progress between rows of bowed heads. By now it was clear to everyone that the Prince had exhausted all possible small talk with either of his Russian guests: and Creevey wrote, with sympathy rather than glee. 'All agree that Prinny will die or go mad; he is worn out with fuss, fatigue and rage.'

Yet he spared no effort to make the State Visit a success. The army was drawn up for review by the foreign heads of state in Hyde Park and the fleet assembled off Spithead. No one could remember such a season of entertainment in London; and to show his magnanimity, the Prince Regent commissioned Thomas Lawrence, the most gifted of English portrait painters, to capture the features of all his distinguished guests on canvas, thereby committing himself to paying £525 for the likeness of a man he had come to hate (though, understandably, Grand Duchess Catherine was not among those favoured by the Regent's artistic patronage). It all made little difference: nothing could ease the antipathy between the Russians and their English host. His own position was made more difficult by the problems of his private life. The Whigs in the Commons had continued to ask awkward questions throughout the previous two years; they wished to know, not only why the Princess of Wales was not received at Court, but for what reason she was denied the company of her daughter, Princess Charlotte; and there was still a powerful movement in London sympathising with Caroline's misfortunes. She was again cheered whenever she visited Covent Garden or any other theatre; and her exclusion from the festivities of 1814 led to demonstrations in her favour, which neither the Tsar nor the King of Prussia could ignore.

Alexander left Dover on his way back to Russia on 27 June, much to the Prince's relief. There was still time for him to make a bid for popular favour; for on the day after the Tsar's unmourned departure, Wellington arrived in England for the first time since his triumphs in the Peninsula; and once again the Prince Regent exercised his skill as an impresario of victory. He paid a personal tribute to Wellington on 21 July with a grand ball at Carlton House, more elaborate than any celebration before or afterwards. A special brick polygon was erected by Nash outside the Gothic Conservatory: it covered an area as big as Westminster Hall and it was draped with white muslin and hung with mirrors, so that it seemed as if it were a huge tented pavilion. In the centre a bank of flowers concealed two bands, which played from midnight until six in the morning. Rather strangely, the invitations to the ball declared that guests were 'to have the honour of meeting Her Majesty the Queen', and the Regent's mother – frail but formidable at seventy – duly attended the festivities, accompanied by her two unmarried daughters; but there was no doubt that the evening really belonged to Wellington. There was a bust of the Duke so placed that everyone looked at it, and the walls were studded with so many 'Ws' that the tribute embarrassed its principal recipient. Allegorical transparencies decorated the supper marquees; if 'Military Glory' and 'The Overthrow of Tyranny by the Allied Powers' were distinctly Spanish in tone, the inspiration is hardly surprising.

There remained, of course, the common people; and twelve days later they had their night of entertainment. Hyde Park, St James's Park and Green Park were given over to an enormous fête, which celebrated both the coming of Peace and the completion of a hundred years of Hanoverian rule in Britain. There were clusters of fireworks in the parks, a Chinese pagoda, Japanese lanterns and a Temple of Concord, while a mimic battle of Trafalgar was fought out on the Serpentine. One of the sensations was a balloon ascent by James Sadler, a member of a family of intrepid aeronauts, who was carried by a strong west wind across London and Essex to the North Sea coast, where he hastily ripped the gasbag with a knife to save himself from a watery landing. There was a shortage of milk, for the cows in Green Park and Hyde Park were frightened by the commotion, but enterprising publicans from Marylebone and Westminster and St Pancras had moved south and set up beer tents beside the Serpentine; and everyone seems to have enjoyed himself. *The Times* remained a little doubtful of the propriety of the celebrations: for, while the newspaper was pleased that so many people could rejoice at an historic event, it deplored the expense and 'the mummery': 'Alas! alas! to what are we sinking?', it asked with rhetorical dismay. But Londoners, liking beer and circuses, refused to see the fête as a moral question.

Unfortunately they were also reluctant to give credit for these festivities to the Prince Regent, whose family difficulties had by now reached a new low in the public eye. All the summer the Whigs had been pressing Lord Castlereagh (who was Leader of the House of Commons) for an increased allowance to the Princess of Wales, and the discussions had once again made the separation of husband and wife a topic of general conversation. On 30 June Princess Caroline was accorded an annual grant of £50,000 a year, more than twice the allowance she had previously received, but she immediately wrote to the Speaker of the Commons and told him that, so as to ease the taxpayers' burdens, she was prepared to accept £35,000 a year. This apparent act of generosity was hailed with delight by her partisans inside and outside the Commons, but they were soon discomforted; for at the end of the first week in August she travelled down to Worthing, where the frigate HMS *Jason* had been put at her disposal, and embarked on it for Germany and a period of residence abroad. She declared to those around her that, as the English Court would not give her the honours due to a Princess of Wales, she was content to remain 'Caroline, a happy merry soul'. And for the next six years she did her best to live down to her word.

Caroline's departure, though a considerable relief for the Prince Regent, did not free him from domestic worries. Her last weeks in England coincided with a crisis in the life of Princess Charlotte and its after-effects were to linger on for several months. Ever since the summer of 1812 Charlotte had been a heroine of the Whigs, who turned to her in opposition as they had done to her father in the days of Pitt and Fox.

It is difficult to analyse the Prince's attitude towards his daughter: he spoke sentimentally of her on her birthday and he lavished expensive gifts on her, but when she was a child he never romped with her, as he did with Minnie Seymour. To his sisters he complained that once Charlotte reached adolescence she seemed always to be sulking; and his exaggerated sense of femininity was often affronted by a hoydenish gaucherie which she affected, as if to irritate him. The Queen's comment that young Charlotte was more consciously her mother's daughter than her father's did not incline him to look upon her with any particular favour. Charlotte was a tragic and often lonely figure: she had no strong feelings for or against either of her parents, both of whom treated her badly though not intentionally. She was contemptuous of those graces in her father's nature which pleased other women; and she pitied her mother as much for the failings of her character as for the slights she had allegedly sustained. Father and daughter were united in one respect: both believed she should make an early marriage, but their concepts of an ideal husband remained far apart.

At the end of 1813 the Prince Regent authorised Castlereagh, as Foreign Secretary, to make arrangements with the ruler of the Netherlands for a marriage between Princess Charlotte and the heir to the Dutch throne, William, Hereditary Prince of Orange (a great-grandfather of Queen Juliana). Such a dynastic union would link the United Kingdom of Britain and Ireland with the projected new Kingdom of a United Netherlands (Belgium, Holland and Luxemburg); and the proposed marriage was therefore of considerable political importance. Charlotte met William shortly before her eighteenth birthday and told a confidante that she considered herself engaged to him, although the marriage contract was not drawn up until the spring of 1814. By then Charlotte no longer felt attracted to 'the Young Frog' (if, indeed, she ever had been) and she made it clear to her father and to her friends in Parliament that she did not think it right for the heir presumptive of England to reside abroad, as William wished. Her opposition to the marriage hardened during the visit of the foreign dignitaries for three reasons: mischievous intrigues of Grand Duchess Catherine and Lady Jersey; the attractions of other more handsome suitors; and obvious failings in William's own character. Every gossip that summer was busy relating tales of his drunken escapades, notably after Ascot Races on 10 June, and Charlotte seems to have had personal experience of his

71

least agreeable habits. On 16 June she informed William by letter that she considered the engagement ended; but her father refused to abandon a marriage project of such importance, and he continued to cajole her into accepting the unfortunate William. The strain severely taxed Charlotte's health. Eventually on 12 July she slipped out of her residence in Warwick House by the backstairs, hailed a hackney cab from a rank at Charing Cross and fled to her mother's home in Connaught Place, where she sought advice from the Whigs. Very sensibly, Brougham urged her to return to Carlton House and there was a tearful reconciliation between father and daughter. The Regent, for the moment, gave up any idea of an Orange marriage and packed Charlotte off to Cranbourne Lodge in Windsor, whence she moved later to Weymouth for the sea-bathing which all the family believed to be a natural cure for every ill. Although the Regent thought it best to change the composition of her household, he did not treat his daughter unkindly and she was permitted to come back to London to say farewell to her mother before she left for the Continent. But popular feeling, excited by the incident of the hackney cab and by tales of the Princess running distraught down Warwick Street, insisted on regarding the Regent as a heartless bully.

Charlotte behaved well at Windsor, as the Queen informed her father. The girl momentarily thought herself in love with the Crown Prince of Prussia, for whom many hearts throbbed that year, although she was not entirely indifferent to Prince Leopold of Saxe-Coburg. They had met several times during the midsummer celebrations, but Leopold may have lessened himself in her eyes by writing, very correctly, to the Regent to assure him of his good intentions towards his daughter. As yet the Prince remained uninterested in the Saxe-Coburgs. He preferred to let Charlotte recover her poise and good sense before discussing with her the awkward question of marriage. She spent Christmas with her father, her aunts, her grandmother and indeed her poor demented grandfather at Windsor; and on Christmas Day itself she caused a major sensation by casually telling the Regent and Princess Mary that she had 'witnessed many things in her mother's room which she could not repeat' and that in 1813 her mother had encouraged her to be a close friend of Captain Hesse, an officer in the Light Dragoons who was commonly thought to be the Duke of York's bastard. She had first encountered him while out riding at Windsor and subsequently her mother had arranged meetings for them in her apartments at Kensington Palace, occasionally leaving them together in a bedroom and locking the door after her. 'God knows what would have become of me if he had not behaved with so much respect to me,' she said, with almost too disarming an air of innocence. They had continued to correspond, with her mother as an intermediary, but Captain Hesse was now one of her mother's aides on the Continent and, as Charlotte said to Princess Mary a few days later, 'she never could make out whether Captain Hesse was her lover or her mother's'. The Prince declared that he would not reproach her but that he would take steps 'to prevent the possibility of such a thing ever happening again'.

Charlotte herself had decided by the third week of January 1815, that the best solution for her difficulties was marriage: 'At all events I know that *worse off*, more wretched and unhappy, I *cannot* be than I am now, and after all if I end by marrying Prince L[eopold], I marry the *best* of all those I *have seen*, and that is some satisfaction,' she wrote in a private letter on 23 January. But a month later she discovered, to her dismay, that her father believed the wisest guarantee of her good name was a speedy marriage to her former fiancé, Prince William of Orange. Once again she took up her pen and sent the Regent a firm note from Cranbourne: 'I candidly allow that a matrimonial connexion would not only be most desirable but be the most likely expedient to remove me from the unpleasant circumstances in which I am placed. But notwithstanding this, I *cannot* indeed comply with your wishes for marrying the Prince of Orange.' To his credit, her father dropped the proposal. Charlotte remained for most of the year at Windsor, although she spent a few dull weeks at Warwick House during the spring. Occasionally letters reached her from Leopold in Vienna and later in Paris; and others told her how bravely Prince William fought at Waterloo and how a marriage was arranged for him with the Tsar's youngest sister. Charlotte showed little interest.

The Regent had more pressing matters on his mind than finding a husband acceptable to his daughter. Early in March there was serious rioting in London as a protest against the Corn Bill, which prohibited the importation of foreign corn if the home price was below eighty shillings a quarter; and on 7 March two Londoners were killed by the soldiery as a mob attacked a Tory minister's home less than half a mile from Carlton House. The Regent thought the Corn Bill a political error, but he regarded any violent demonstration as proof of incipient Jacobinism and he approved, on this occasion and later, of the firm stand made by the Liverpool Government. Though personally humane and anxious always to mitigate severe judicial penalties, the Regent fully shared the common fear of 'Revolution', for he could never rid his mind of the refugees he had found flocking to Brighton in 1792.

The London riots coincided with alarming reports from the Continent: Napoleon had fled from Elba, landed in southern France and was marching on Paris to oust Louis XVIII. Most of the Allied sovereigns and statesmen were gathered in Congress at Vienna and they at once issued a declaration branding 'Buonaparte' an international outlaw. When news of Napoleon's gamble reached London, Castlereagh had just arrived back from Vienna and his knowledge of the European situation helped the Regent and the Government to face the crisis calmly. Wellington, himself in Vienna, was appointed to command the army in the Low Countries and left for Brussels at the end of March. Everyone was convinced that should Napoleon cross the new frontiers of France, his power would be swiftly broken: and the Regent shared the general confidence in Wellington's ability.

It would, however, be a mistake to assume that during these 'Hundred Days' the Regent's thoughts were concentrated solely on military matters. In 1812 he had commissioned Nash to construct a Royal Lodge in Windsor Great Park and the 'cottage', as he called it, was now ready for occupation. Its completion enabled Nash to begin work on a project long dear to the Prince's heart, the reshaping of the classical exterior of Henry Holland's Pavilion in Brighton so as to give it an Indian design. The interior decoration had assumed a Chinese character as early as 1803, and work had continued every year on the general fabric; but during his visit to the Pavilion in the autumn of 1814, the Prince thought the building cramped and he authorised Nash to undertake a major project which would give him more rooms while, at the same time, stamping the external appearance of his favourite home with individual genius. Inspiration came to Nash – or, more precisely, in the first instance to Humphrey Repton, who was closely associated with Nash – from Sezincote, a country house near Moreton-in-Marsh, built in Hindu style for a retired administrator in the East India Company. Nash started his labours at Brighton in March 1815 and

74

twice during that summer the Regent came down to bustle the work-
men, who seemed to him deplorably slow. Enough progress was made
for a large party at Christmas, but it was not until the summer of
1818 that the famous Oriental dome was added, an architectural
transformation which prompted William Wilberforce's famous observation that 'the Dome of St Paul's must have come down to Brighton
and pupped'. The whole work on the external fabric took five years and
the project cost nearly £150,000, exclusive of interior furnishings.

In 1812 Byron had written caustically:

> Shut up – no, not the King, – but the Pavilion,
> Or else 'twill cost us all another million.

The prediction, though exaggerated, put into verse a fear which continued to excite Whigs and radicals throughout the Regency decade.
Each spring, as the Civil List came up for debate in the Commons, the
Government had trouble with Opposition spokesmen over the Prince's
extravagance. On 8 May 1815, Lord Castlereagh was forced to use considerable debating skill in defending the Regent's failure to keep his
expenditure within the estimates. At two o'clock the following morning
Castlereagh sent a weary note to the Prince informing him that he had
defeated the Whig attacks. He added, however, that he 'had the morti-
fication of observing many of the friends of Government, either vote
against, or go away'; and he politely begged the Regent to avoid
committing himself to such 'fluctuating charges', since 'these annual
discussions on Civil List questions are untremely prejudicial to the best
interests and authority of the Crown'. The warning was well merited
but his words had little effect; over such matters the Prince was in-
corrigible.

At the start of June he was delighted to be able to stay, for the first
time, in what the Whigs termed 'the thatched palace' at Windsor. It
was Ascot Week, but the Prince found few of his friends at the races
that year: most of the aristocratic regiments were in Belgium, where
everyone anticipated a great battle. By the middle of the month the
Regent was back in London and, on the evening of 21 June, he attended
a ball given by the wife of a merchant-banker, Mrs Boehm, in St James's
Square. Most people of consequence were present: the Duke of York,
Lord Alvanley, Lord Liverpool, Lord Castlereagh, Mr Canning among

them. They were awaiting dinner when suddenly there was a strange apparition at the door. A weary figure in a major's uniform stood clasping the poles of Napoleonic eagles. He had brought the first despatches and trophies of Waterloo. The Regent, his brother and most of the Government retired to study the news from Wellington; and when they came back to the dining-room it was seen that tears were running down the Prince's cheeks. No one doubted that Wellington had won a decisive victory and it was assumed that the Prince's grief (which brought an abrupt end to the evening's festivities) sprang from sorrow at the familiar names he had seen on the casualty list. There may well, however, have been another reason for his deep emotion. On the evening of 18 June, the 'Tenth or Prince Regent's Own Royal Hussars' had charged forward on the French positions around the wayside inn known as *La Belle Alliance*; and they sustained such remarkably light losses that, with the French cavalry in flight before them, they broke through to the squares of the Imperial Old Guard. Thus, by a strange freak of fortune, the Tenth Hussars – so often lampooned by the Prince's enemies at home – distinguished themselves in the final action of the most renowned of Napoleon's regiments. The Regent knew the Hussars and their officers so well that they seemed to him part of his person; and it is small wonder if, in later years, he believed he had himself been present on the field of Waterloo.

6

Marriages and Mourning
1815–19

Waterloo was won: and by the time the news reached London the campaign was already over. For the Regent, however, it was to have a strange epilogue. On 13 July Napoleon, who had sought refuge at the Atlantic port of Rochefort, sent him a carefully worded request for asylum before surrendering to the Captain of HMS *Bellerophon*:

> Pursued by the factions which divide my country and by the hostility of the greatest European powers [Napoleon wrote] I have ended my political career and I come, as Themistocles did, to seat myself at the hearth of the British people. I put myself under the protection of its laws, which I claim from Your Royal Highness as the strongest, most consistent and most generous of my foes.

Such an appeal was by no means the wild gambler's throw it appears in retrospect. Predictably the Regent was flattered by its tone of respect: 'Upon my soul,' he said when he read it, 'a very proper letter – much more so, I must say, than any I ever received from Louis XVIII.' At least one of the Regent's brothers (the Duke of Sussex) had some sympathy for the fallen Emperor and even Castlereagh seriously considered if it were possible to keep him under some form of dignified restraint in Scotland rather than transport him to distant exile. Though long the bogey man of cautionary nursery tales, Napoleon in defeat exercised a curious fascination over the English public and a government less frightened by popular demonstration might well have shown magnanimity. But Lord Liverpool was not prepared to take the risk of confining Napoleon within the British Isles lest his presence might encourage those who despaired of the existing order. The Regent accordingly made no formal reply to the new Themistocles; and by the fourth week in July there were rumours in London that Napoleon was to be sent to St Helena. Lady Anne Barnard, writing to the Prince as 'a dutiful subject and affectionate friend', insisted on forwarding six sketches she had drawn on St Helena a few years earlier, but the Regent did not feel moved to interfere on behalf of 'that feeble bird . . . who has flown for shelter to your nest' (as Lady Anne rather oddly described the ex-Emperor of the French). On 8 August HMS *Northumberland*, to which 'General Bonaparte' was transferred from the *Bellerophon*, left Torbay for the South Atlantic; and, as Napoleon sailed from Europe into legend, the 'most consistent' of his enemies turned to the familiar trivialities of life at Carlton House, and the Cottage at Windsor, and the fantasy Pavilion by the sea.

His relations with his daughter – and, indeed, with all the Royal Family – were far better in the closing months of 1815 than they had been for many years. Charlotte was deeply hurt by her mother's abrupt departure at a time of crisis in her own life and she was shocked by the tales that reached her from the Continent. For, though Caroline had passed a few weeks in Brunswick, she had speedily made her way southwards to Milan and Naples, where she spent several months of the winter of 1814–15 revelling in Joachim Murat's Court. So scandalous was her conduct that the Privy Council in London solemnly advised the Regent that if the Princess of Wales ever sought to return to England 'she was not to be admitted' to the country; and her daughter inevitably drew closer to the father she had so long despised. Shortly before Christmas Charlotte and the Prince had an affectionate meeting, during which he appears to have told her that she might make her own choice of husband from a number of possible princes; and later that same day she wrote to her father, 'Thus encouraged I no longer hesitate in declaring my partiality in favour of the Prince of Coburg – assuring you no one will be more steady or consistent in this their present and last engagement than myself.' Castlereagh, for political reasons, strongly favoured a marriage to Leopold of Saxe-Coburg and was entrusted by the Regent with the task of negotiating the arrangements; and an invitation duly went out to Leopold at the end of January 1816 for him to come to England and claim his bride.

Before his arrival the Regent spent a happy month in Brighton. For

78

the first time in eleven years he invited Princess Charlotte to stay at the Pavilion, where she celebrated her twentieth birthday as one of a large house-party, which included the Queen and two of her unmarried aunts. The Dowager Countess of Ilchester, a leading member of Charlotte's household, wrote an account of the visit which includes one of the most detailed descriptions of life at the Pavilion:

> The fortnight at Brighton has had a very happy effect on Princess Charlotte's spirits and she has an air of cheerful content . . . The Chinese scene is gay beyond description . . . Every one was free in the morning of all Court restraint, and only met at six o'clock punctually for dinner to the number of between thirty and forty, and in the evening about as many more were generally invited; a delightful band of music played till half-past eleven, when the Royal Family took their leave, and the rest of the company also, after partaking of sandwiches. The evenings were not the least formal. As soon as the Queen sat down to cards everybody moved about as they pleased, and made their own backgammon, chess or card party, but the walking up and down the gallery was the favourite lounge. All the rooms open into this beautiful gallery, which is terminated at each end by the lightest and prettiest Chinese staircases you can imagine, made of cast-iron and bamboo, with glass doors beneath, which reflect the gay lanterns at each end . . . Each staircase communicates to a large room . . . The effect of this centrical common room is very good. There was in it an excellent fire and books and newspapers.

It was upon this curious scene that Prince Leopold descended on 23 February, to find the Regent so ill with gout that he could only move down the long corridors in a wheeled chair. A few days later Charlotte returned to Brighton and the courtship proceeded decorously under the eagle-eyes of the Queen and Lady Ilchester. It was a genuine love-match, with Leopold (a solemn and dutiful young man of twenty-six) patiently taming Charlotte's wilder manners. They were married on 2 May 1816, in London. 'When the ceremony was over,' the Prime Minister's wife reported to her sister, 'the Princess knelt to her father for his blessing, which he gave her, and then raised her and gave her a good hearty, paternal hug that delighted me.' The Prince permitted them to set up home at Claremont, near Esher in Surrey, and Parliament rather surprisingly voted Leopold a pension of £50,000 a year (which was even to continue should the Princess die). There was no doubt of Charlotte's popularity.

None of it, however, seems to have encompassed her father as well. The cartoonists did not spare him in his attack of gout and, shortly before the wedding, *The Times* printed a detailed account of how the Regent had to be hoisted into the saddle of his horse after being wheeled up an inclined plane to a platform 'which was then raised high enough to pass the horse under'. Caricaturists could not resist such a ludicrous operation, especially when it took place against the mock-Oriental background of the Pavilion. None of these shafts of wit, unkind though they were, mattered very much; but the renewed attacks on the Regent's extravagance were more significant, for the contrast between his reckless quest for luxurious living and the poverty of the labouring masses inevitably bred resentment. In the spring of 1816 one Whig member of Parliament was so indignant at what he believed life was like at Brighton that he told the Commons he wished to hear 'no more of that squanderous and lavish profusion which in a certain quarter resembled more the pomp and magnificence of a Persian satrap seated in all the splendour of Oriental state, than the sober dignity of a British Prince, seated in the bosom of his subjects'.

The Government could not ignore the mood of back-benchers in both parties; and on 15 March 1816 a joint plea was sent to the Regent in the names of the Prime Minister, the Leader of the Commons, and the Chancellor of the Exchequer. They begged him to ensure 'that all new expenses for additions or alterations at Brighton or elsewhere will, under the present circumstances, be abandoned'. As so often he made gestures of economy, a momentary pause in the royal spending spree, and he was helped by a gift of £50,000 from the Queen towards the 'Splendid improvements' at Brighton; but there was no real attempt at cheese-paring. The upkeep of the band, which delighted his guests every evening and played for them at each ball, was £6,000 a year exclusive of uniforms; and when the Music Room in the Pavilion was given the Nash treatment of 'decorating and furnishing' the total cost amounted to no less than £45,125.

Money spent by the Prince Regent on the purchase and commissioning of paintings and other works of art was, of course, an investment;

but the increasing amounts spent on food and entertainment are hard to justify at a time when the Corn Laws made starvation a real threat in many country districts throughout the land. For several months in the winter of 1816–17 the Regent employed the finest of all French chefs, Marie-Antoine Carème, to prepare the dinners at Carlton House and at Brighton. His dishes were in themselves noble essays of imaginative skill, and they were presented in a menu which was a masterpiece of balanced composition. Questions of food and wine were topics of major concern to the Regent, who discussed them with Carème and his other master-chefs; and he was equally determined that any ball should be as well-staged as a dramatic production. The Regent's sense of hospitality is well-illustrated by the visit which Grand Duke Nicholas of Russia, later Tsar Nicholas I, made to the Royal Pavilion in the third week of January 1817. On the first night Carème produced for the Grand Duke and the Regent's other guests a menu of one hundred dishes served in nine courses. There was a ball on the following night, which the Grand Duke opened with Minnie Seymour as his partner. As he was only twenty years old and therefore too young to have fought in the wars, he delighted in wearing military uniform, and his host and fellow guests duly appeared in full regimentals. When the Grand Duke asked for that ballroom novelty, a waltz, to be played, the band at once obliged, even though it was too energetic a dance for the most familiar figures in Brighton Society. It is interesting that the Regent should have taken such care of the Grand Duke's comfort, for he intensely disliked Nicholas's brother (Tsar Alexander) and his sister Catherine. He was, however, always conscious of his obligations as a host; and he was generous to guests, whether they were arrogant young Romanovs, or tedious bores from the noblest families, or the principal patron of the Society for the Suppression of Vice and the Encouragement of Religion and Virtue, William Wilberforce MP (who was a little surprised to find himself invited to dine at the Pavilion while on a visit of good works to Brighton). But most of the Regent's subjects knew little of the urbane civility in which he tried to live out middle age. They believed Carlton House and the Pavilion to be dens of iniquity where the wealthier landowners abandoned themselves to orgies. With unemployment and repression stalking the land, Lord Liverpool's Government genuinely feared a wave of seditious republicanism. There was a demonstration in Spa Fields, London, in November 1816 at which someone noticed a 'cap of liberty' mounted on a pike, and tricolour flags were waved defiantly by one section of the crowd. Gloomy observers, thinking of Carlton House on one side of the capital and Spa Fields on the other, were reminded of Paris 'in the year '89'.

Twelve days after the ball at Brighton in honour of the Grand Duke, all this discontent moved dramatically to the surface. On 28 January 1817 the Regent formally opened a new session of Parliament. As he was returning down the Mall to Carlton House angry demonstrators threw stones at his coach. A round hole was found in the window and it was believed that a shot had been fired at him, from an air-gun. The Regent at once declared that an attempt had been made to assassinate him. A solemn prayer was offered on the following Sunday in churches throughout the Kingdom for the 'protection of his Royal Person', that he might be shielded 'from the arrow that flieth by day and from the pestilence that walketh in darkness'. The prayer, it would seem, was answered. For, though conditions remained bad and though the repressive laws were intensified, there were no more menacing demonstrations made against the Regent himself. He never became popular and his follies were still derided in the Press, but at least he was immune from open insult and assault. When, on the second anniversary of Waterloo, he opened the new bridge across the Thames which took its name from the victory, some of the crowd cheered as he passed by, although members of his procession did not fail to point out that he was accompanied at the time by the Duke of Wellington. Throughout the spring and summer of 1817 his own spirits remained remarkably cheerful, not least because of the obvious happiness of Charlotte and Leopold at Claremont, where a baby was expected to be born in the third or fourth week of October.

On 27 October, with no news good or bad from Claremont, the Prince Regent left London for the Hertfords' country estate at Sudbourne in Suffolk, where he had been invited to shoot. Princess Charlotte was attended by the most esteemed obstetrician of the day and there seemed no particular reason for concern that the baby should be overdue. But suddenly on Wednesday afternoon, 5 November, the tone of a letter sent from Claremont at ten on the previous night so alarmed the Prince that he drove back to town as fast as tired horses could carry him. His fears were justified. At nine that Wednesday night a still-born son was delivered; and at half-past two in the morning of

6 November Princess Charlotte died. The tragic news was broken to the Regent by the Duke of York less than two hours later. The Prince was overcome with grief and had to be bled in the course of the day; but he insisted on being driven out to Claremont before Charlotte's body was finally laid in the coffin. There was a scene of terrible emotion: his companions found it difficult to calm the Prince or to write an account of their experience; but at last he was escorted back to Carlton House, the blinds of his carriage drawn so as to shelter him from inquisitive eyes. He remained in shattered seclusion until after the funeral, weeping for the daughter he had lost, for the grandchild whom he had hoped would determine the succession, and for the son-in-law on whom he had come to rely for counsel more than his Ministers appreciated (or, indeed, would have desired).

The Regent's loss was shared deeply by the nation. Ever since her marriage – and, to some extent, even earlier – Princess Charlotte had been the darling of the people, a talisman of a happier future embodying hopes for the nineteenth century, in which almost all her conscious life was spent. Inevitably, amid the sincere sense of bereavement, people pointed accusing fingers at those whom they considered responsible for the tragedy. The competence of Sir Richard Croft, her obstetrician, was questioned: why had he kept the Princess short of food? why had he allowed her to be weakened by anaemia? why had he left her bedside so soon after the delivery of her stillborn child? Although both the Regent and Prince Leopold publicly cleared him from blame, he was so reviled that eighteen months later he committed suicide. Nor was he the only target. There was anger that no female member of the Royal Family was present at Claremont and that the Prince Regent should have been enjoying himself with Lady Hertford at such a critical moment in his daughter's life. Old tales of neglect were once more bandied around.

Shortly after the funeral the Regent went down to Brighton, where he spent three months in deep mourning. He seems to have suffered a physical and nervous breakdown, which he described to the Queen as 'a sort of mishmash, Solomongrundy, Olla podrida kind of a business that is quite anomalous'. He retired early to bed, dismissed his band (thereby, incidentally, saving some £2,000) and became careless about his appearance. He shed the corsets which restricted his girth: 'Prinny has let loose his belly which now reaches to his knees', wrote Lord

Folkestone early in the New Year to Creevey. But at Christmas he began to pick up affairs of State and to attend to difficulties within the family. His three unmarried brothers – the Dukes of Clarence, Kent and Cambridge – had considered taking wives even before the tragedy at Claremont, for dynastic marriages held a prospect of increased allowances from Parliament and the settlement of debts. Clarence, now in his fifty-third year, had been in the habit of proposing marriage to eligible princesses at frequent intervals ever since 1814, when he had even paid court to the Grand Duchess Catherine. Provided that his funded debt of £40,000 and his floating debt of £16,000 were settled and that there were adequate guarantees for the ten Fitzclarence children, to whom he was a 'fond and attached father', he had no objection at all to marriage; and his brothers were similarly prepared to abandon mistresses in favour of regular domesticity. The air of 1818 was heavy with belated nuptials: the Duke of Cambridge married Augusta of Hesse-Cassel on 7 May; the Duke of Kent married Prince Leopold's sister, Victoria of Leiningen, on 29 May; and the Duke of Clarence, having caused consternation in January by proposing to an English commoner who happened to be a wealthy heiress, was married on 11 July to Adelaide of Saxe-Meiningen. Their sister, Princess Elizabeth, had already set the fashion by marrying the Prince of Hesse-Homburg in April. Cruikshank and other caricaturists, their pens softened by the sorrows of November, took heart again: so long as George III's offspring lived, there was no fear that any cartoonist would lack material for satire.

Meanwhile Princess Caroline continued to shock European society. Soon after her departure from England in 1814 she had appointed as 'cabinet-courier' (secretary) an obscure Italian veteran of Napoleon's Russian campaign, Bartolomeo Pergami, who encouraged her to purchase an attractive villa – which she named the Villa d'Este – on the shores of Lake Como. Pergami became her constant companion, not only in Italy, but on her frequent journeys through the German lands and farther afield. She was a strangely restless woman, with an insatiable curiosity for the mysterious Orient and it was this wanderlust which carried her in 1816 to the Greek islands, to Constantinople, and ultimately to Jericho. She was not the type of person who delights in travelling incognito: when she reached the Holy Land she insisted on riding into Jerusalem at the head of a considerable retinue, with twenty-five close attendants and nearly two hundred opportunists trailing behind; and while she was in Jerusalem she suddenly instituted a new knightly fraternity of chivalry, the Order of St Caroline, of which Pergami was inevitably created Grand Master. Some months later, back in Italy, she gave Pergami the title of Baron and formally appointed him Chamberlain of her Household.

A wish-fulfilment Court, such as Caroline established, is always a pathetic institution, but not necessarily morally reprehensible. It was Caroline's attempts to draw attention to herself and to her little world which created the scandals. Thus we hear of the Princess of Wales sleeping like a latterday Cleopatra under a tent on the deck of a polacca, with Pergami's quarters close by, through a painted canvas door; or we see her posing for a portrait as the repentant Magdalene, 'her person very much exposed'; or driving through Genoa, at the age of fifty, in a low-cut bodice and short white skirt, with a pink hat and pink feathers; or arriving at the opera in Baden noisily and late, dressed like an Alpine peasant at a flower festival, with ribbons streaming from her thick black hair and spangles flashing above her coarse reddened cheeks. No one doubted that the private moments of her life matched these public images in vulgar absurdity. Small wonder that the Prince Regent thought seriously of divorcing the woman he had so long loathed. Even Whigs like Creevey believed her conduct over the previous five years provided ample material for divorce.

In August 1818 the Regent accordingly accepted a proposal from Sir John Leach, one of his law officers, that a three-man investigation should be undertaken in Italy to establish the truth about his wife's behaviour. Two barristers and a major from a fashionable regiment constituted what was called 'the Milan Commission', a body which examined several dozen Italian witnesses on oath before reporting, in the following summer, that there was no doubt Caroline was living adulterously with Bartolomeo Pergami. But this information posed new problems for which there seemed no simple solution. The Liverpool Government was reluctant to advise the Regent to begin proceedings for a divorce: ministers feared that any apparent persecution of Caroline would lead to a reaction in her favour; and they were also uncertain over the precise legal form any action might take, for the offences had occurred only on foreign soil and Pergami had never in his life been subject to English law. Had he been British his conduct might well have constituted high treason and carried the severest penalties; but, fortunately, he was not and less drastic measures would have to be employed, or none at all. 'We must always recollect,' wrote Castlereagh, 'that the proceeding, if it be taken, must ultimately be a parliamentary one.' As leader of the Tories in the Commons, he knew that it would be impossible for the Government to rely on support from the back-benches if a wave of sympathy for the Princess suddenly swept the country.

As yet there was, indeed, no sign of it. Only Henry Brougham and his brother James remained active partisans of the Princess at Westminster; and neither of them had any illusions over Caroline's general conduct. James Brougham went to Milan while the Commission was at work. Caroline let him know she was prepared to remain abroad and not claim her rank as Queen-Consort at her husband's accession if she received a satisfactory monetary grant; but she could never accept any form of divorce, nor was she willing to tolerate Parliamentary proceedings which sought to show her as guilty of infidelity. By some extraordinary process of reasoning, she had convinced herself of her innocence of all scandalous conduct. Should her good name be sullied by the Regent and his ministers she was prepared to raise a storm of protest throughout England. With radical demonstrations continuing against the Corn Law and with unemployment growing in north-western England, no political leader wished to excite further controversy. Why provide the dissidents with a heroine? For the moment, the question of a divorce was left unresolved.

While the Milan Commission was still hearing evidence, the Regent was deprived of advice from the one person who really understood the contrasting egoisms in his complex character; for the summer of royal nuptials ended with the not unexpected death of Queen Charlotte, in her seventy-fifth year. The Prince felt the break deeply. Although in his youth she had treated him severely, a close relationship had begun to grow between them ever since he turned to her for consolation at the time of his marriage to Caroline. The final lunacy of George III led Queen Charlotte to seek an interest in the real world, away from the sinister shadows at Windsor where the King still lived out his protracted nightmare existence. The letters which passed between the

Queen and the Regent from 1812 until her death show warm affection and humour: each enjoyed gossip and private jokes, many of them at the expense of the Duke of Clarence, on whose marital affairs the Queen had exercised her habitual talent for interference only five months before her final collapse. The strain had been too much for her weakened constitution and she died on 17 November 1818, at Kew.

This new family loss so depressed the Regent that his own health once more collapsed, and he spent almost a month immured within Carlton House. Though still only in his mid-fifties, he began to seem an old man. That December he admitted to one of his guests at Brighton that he had given up the struggle to mount a horse. 'Why should I?', he added querulously. 'I never had better spirits or appetite than when I stay within.' Yet, as so often, he was deluding himself. There was a sad emptiness in his life that Christmas. He attended, of course, to the ritual festivities: there were new rooms to be shown to his guests at Brighton and a whole range 'of contrivances for roasting, boiling, baking, stewing, frying, steaming and heating' for them to see in the massive kitchen which Nash had recently completed. And, anxious for innovation, the Regent gave a supper to his servants, with a scarlet cloth thrown across the tables in the kitchen so that 'the good-humoured Prince' could spend 'a joyous hour' below stairs in appropriate state. But, to the penetrating eye, it was clear that much was missing from the scene. No more dandies: they had never recovered from the disgrace, bankruptcy and flight to Calais of Brummell to escape his debtors in 1816. No more long hours of gambling: Sheridan, the last of the Prince's 'boon companions', had died impoverished two years before, an ornate public funeral the final gesture of theatre in his life. No more grand reviews of the military, though the Tenth Hussars remained available for 'duties at Court' when they were not rounding up smugglers at Shoreham and Worthing. He had lost so many friends by death or disinclination: little was seen of Lady Hertford after the tragedy of poor Charlotte; and, though Mrs Fitzherbert still lived in Brighton and some believed she might bloom once more in society, she never visited the Pavilion again until after he was dead. Another friend from the Prince's youth had now gone from the scene. For, in April 1818, Lady Melbourne, the supreme hostess of the years of elegance, died in London. She had remained close to the Prince ever since they had first danced and laughed and loved, a third of a century ago. He grieved so deeply for Betsy Melbourne that four years later he still shed a tear as he reminded her daughter, Emily Cowper, of how he had walked across to Melbourne House almost daily during that final illness, and of how Lady Melbourne had passed away in his arms. It was a touching tale but an odd reminiscence, as Lady Cowper knew full well; for in those days she had rarely left her mother's bedside, and not once had the Regent come near her.

There were still pleasures which the Regent enjoyed. He read considerably in the winter of 1818–19, and was delighted with the historical romances of Walter Scott, whom he created a baronet early in 1819. And the Prince's judgment and patronage of the visual arts was undiminished. But evening after evening there was an atmosphere of frustrated boredom, both at the Pavilion and at Carlton House. He sang, he listened, he talked, he played whist and solitaire: but he did not actually rule. One evening at the Pavilion a guest noticed his host quietly playing patience, and was amused to observe that, however the cards came up, the Regent could never quite get the King out. And so it was in real life; the reign of George IV was an unconscionable time a-coming.

7
Royal George 1819–22

The sixtieth year of the reign of George III began in October 1819 with no apparent change in the King's condition. He was a pathetic figure, deaf and blind and mad, a bearded octogenarian who held conversations with his predecessors and strummed tunelessly hour by hour on a harpsichord in the gloom at Windsor. Few people thought of him, and yet everyone accepted his existence as part of the natural order, since hardly any of his subjects could remember a different sovereign on the throne of England. It seemed as if he would survive as long as the crumbling stones of the medieval castle around him; and so indeed he might – except that, in the first weeks of 1820, he unaccountably decided to give up eating and wasted away. At half-past eight in the evening of 29 January he breathed his last with the Duke of York at his bedside. A wave of sympathy and affection, tinged with bewilderment and apprehension, swept across the southern counties of England, as if a familiar tree had been felled by lightning.

At first it looked as if the longest reign of an English king was to be succeeded by the shortest. King George IV was proclaimed 'solely and rightfully' ruler of his British domains by the Garter King of Arms at noon on 31 January in the forecourt of Carlton House. He had been unwell for some days and the sudden emergence from over-heated rooms to a sunny but bitterly cold ceremony brought on an alarming attack of pleurisy. By the evening of 1 February he was said to be in 'imminent danger' of death. Medical bulletins were issued at night and morning for the remainder of the week, and his doctors insisted on draining one hundred and fifty fluid ounces of blood from his system in order to save his life. Although George III's funeral did not take place until 15 February, the new King's medical advisers urged him not to attend it, as the emotional stress of such a 'dangerous effort of respect and piety' might lead to a relapse in his own condition. Accordingly he travelled down to Brighton for a protracted convalescence of two months. It is as well he did not go to Windsor for the funeral: it was a day of dense fog, with the Great Park gripped in icy clamminess; and it would almost certainly have overtaxed the King's constitution.

His convalescence was not, however, peaceful. If he was now King, then Caroline was Queen-Consort; and this posed urgent problems. How was the prayer for the Royal Family to be worded in the Anglican liturgy? What part, if any, should Caroline play in the coronation ceremonies? What advice should be given to foreign courts discreetly enquiring about the honours they should accord Caroline in her interminable journeyings? The King had no doubt of the answer to every question: Church and State should ignore the existence of a Queen-Consort while the King's Ministers found a speedy method of divorce. But the Cabinet insisted that they could not introduce a Bill of Divorce without evidence being heard by judges in an ecclesiastical court and that, if the Queen decided to fight for her rights, it was likely that 'recriminations of every kind' would be made; and, though this was left unsaid, His Majesty's subjects would be treated to unedifying details of their new sovereign's relations with Maria Fitzherbert, Lady Jersey, Lady Hertford and all his long line of matriarchs, living and dead. Understandably, the King was displeased and he seems seriously to have considered dismissing the Government and finding a more compliant set of Ministers; but it was by no means clear where he would discover them. No other Tories could have tried so hard to accommodate his wishes as the existing Cabinet, and the Whigs would never accept responsibility for piloting a divorce through the Commons. Reluctantly the King had to agree to the Government's suggestions that Caroline be granted an annuity payable only so long as she remained abroad and on the understanding that her name should be omitted from the prayer-book and that she would not expect the honour of coronation. George IV, after a quarter of a century of dealing with Caroline, doubted if she would accept such conditions. His Ministers were more optimistic. They hoped the new reign might at least open quietly.

There was never a chance that it would. In the previous year demands for political reform had swept the country but, far from making concessions, the Tory Government hardened its heart. In July 1819 there was trouble in Birmingham, a growing city still without Parliamentary representation, and a month later the local magistrates in Manchester lost their nerve when fifty thousand people assembled at a reform rally in St Peter's Fields, and sent in the local Yeomanry: the subsequent 'Peterloo Massacre' claimed eleven dead and four hundred injured, and it created a legend of popular resistance to government tyranny. Radical feeling intensified during the winter of 1819–20 while Liverpool's Ministry introduced more repressive measures. Within four weeks of George IV's accession a group of conspirators were seized in Cato Street, Marylebone (off the Edgware Road), as they were planning to murder the entire Cabinet and to provoke a general insurrection in the capital. Although the wretched conspirators were dupes of a government spy, their trial in April was so full of the menace of revolution that it sent apprehensive shivers through polite London society. When five of them were publicly executed in the City on May Day, it was thought advisable to close each end of the Old Bailey with a troop of Horse Guards lest the spectacle of hanging and subsequent decapitation might provoke the mob to violence.

It was in this tense atmosphere that Queen Caroline returned to claim her rights. By mid-May it was known that she was on her way back through Switzerland and, at the end of the month, she had the effrontery to send a letter to the Prime Minister asking for the royal yacht to be made ready at Calais to receive her on 3 June. The request was refused. But on 5 June she crossed the Channel and was welcomed in Dover with excitement as great as when Wellington arrived triumphant from Spain in 1814. The prospect of the imminent return of a woman wronged by King and Government threw Londoners into a frenzy of muddled loyalties and protests. Alderman Wood, twice Lord Mayor, emerged as campaign manager in a bid for popular support. On 7 June he greeted her outside London, offering her hospitality in his home in South Audley Street. She was cheered across Westminster Bridge and, as her landau passed Carlton House, the sentries at once presented arms. It was too good a dramatic moment for Caroline to miss: 'Long live the King!', she cried, as her carriage swept down Pall Mall. Her husband was not at home to hear her.

In retrospect it is clear that Caroline rendered her one service to the nation by coming back to London at such a troubled time. Cheering the Queen's cause was a simpler emotional response for a mob of demonstrators than shouting 'Liberty and Reform' or 'Universal Suffrage'; and genuine political and social grievances became submerged in a crusade for the rights of a courageous woman who seemed to be victimised by 'the System'. Naturally, at the time, the King did not appreciate that the new and more vociferous mood of the people was less of a menace than the monster rallies of the previous summer. He stayed away from London for fear of hostile demonstrations and received daily reports from the Home Secretary on the temper of the capital. For six months, from the long days of a scorching midsummer to the dreary fogs of November, the Queen's affairs absorbed the attentions of the nation. No one emerged with credit from this sordid business, but equally no one was prepared to die for Caroline's rights. The barricades of revolt may be raised by high tragedy, but never by vulgar farce. What was wrongly termed 'the Queen's Trial' provided a safety-valve for popular discontent.

While it lasted, it was undoubtedly good theatre. At the end of June 1820 the Government prepared a Bill of Pains and Penalties, an archaic means of using the machinery of Parliament to establish wrongs without resort to the formal proofs essential in a court of law. Had the Bill passed through Lords and Commons, and received the royal assent, it would have deprived 'Her Majesty Caroline Amelia Elizabeth . . . of the title of Queen' and declared her marriage to the King 'for ever wholly dissolved, annulled and made void'. The proceedings, which dragged on for eleven weeks, were strictly limited to the alleged adulterous relationship between Caroline and Pergami; and it was thus hoped that there would be no opportunity for the Queen's attorney-general, Henry Brougham, to throw discredit on her husband's fidelity or to raise other questions of even greater embarrassment concerning Maria Fitzherbert. Almost every peer and bishop, together with most of the judges in the realm, were required to attend the 'trial' which was held in an annexe to the House of Lords, specially constructed for the occasion. The Queen was allowed to be present but not to give evidence. Sometimes she went to the hearing, although often she was content to remain in an adjoining room playing backgammon with Alderman Wood, while the most distinguished gathering in England heard intimate details of her private moments. 'Never, in all my life, have I spent two more unpleasant hours,' remarked Wellington to a friend after one of the earliest sessions. And the credibility of the Italian witnesses raised scorn throughout the country. '*Non mi ricordo*' ('I do not recollect') was a stock answer of one confidential servant to Brougham's cross-examination. The phrase soon passed into the English idiom as a means of not expressing facts convenient to forget.

The Queen stayed at Brandenburg House in Hammersmith or at 15 St James's Square (Castlereagh lived at no. 18) while the proceedings were being heard in the Lords. She turned her journeys across London into proud progresses, in which she was hailed as 'The Queen, The Queen' by madly excited partisans along the route. Someone chalked on the walls of the Russian Embassy, 'The Queen for ever! The King in the river!' and there was an epidemic of obscene graffiti around Carlton House and Pall Mall. The King remained in his 'cottage' at Windsor, where he was consoled by the latest grandmother to become a royal favourite, the Marchioness of Conyngham, to whom he had first formed an attachment the previous Christmas. He was distressed by the sordid revelations with which the Lords Spiritual and Temporal found their time preoccupied and he blamed Liverpool for resorting to such a public method of obtaining a separation from his wife, especially since by the beginning of September the Prime Minister wished to drop 'the four last lines of the Bill, which enacted the divorce, and by inference would enable Your Majesty to marry again'. It was reasonable of the King to complain that if his Ministers did not think they could steer the Bill through Parliament, they should never have proposed such a measure; and it was equally reasonable for Liverpool to contend that the Cabinet had always been opposed to raising the question of divorce and that the Bill had been drafted to satisfy the King. The whole affair was ill-conceived and clumsily handled. On 7 October the King wrote sadly to his brother, the Duke of York,

Though I have now lived a good many years in the world, still I never thought that I should have lived to witness so much prevarication, so much lying, and so much wilful and convenient forgetfulness . . . For certain it is a very strange world that we do now live in where everyone now thinks he has a right to say if he pleases, and in defiance of all truth and reason, that black is white and white is black.

Inevitably the evidence against Caroline was circumstantial and, though no more than a handful of peers considered her innocent, a considerable number disliked the whole procedure. Lawyers thought it offended the principles of equity; the archbishops and bishops were troubled over the divorce issue. The uncertainties became clear when, after the hearing of evidence ended on 24 October, the matter was subject to debate in the House, as any other measure would have been. On 6 November a vote was taken in the Lords on the second reading of the Bill: the Government majority was twenty-eight. Four days later came the crucial vote on the third reading; and now the majority fell to nine. Liverpool knew that this was tantamount to defeat. Had the Bill gone to the Commons, it would almost certainly have been rejected and the Government would have fallen. Rather than risk a full debate in the lower House, Liverpool at once withdrew the Bill; and Parliament was immediately prorogued for a fortnight until the political situation became clearer.

There was widespread rejoicing in London and many other cities. The capital was 'illuminated' for three nights, as it had been after the fall of Paris. The Queen enjoyed a fortnight of popularity. Alderman Wood suggested that there should be a solemn service of thanksgiving in St Paul's Cathedral for the deliverance of the Queen from her enemies. The Church dignitaries did not feel obliged to assist Caroline to fulfil this particular religious duty; but the Dean and Chapter were embarrassed by the support given to the Queen by the Lord Mayor of London and by several prominent members of the Corporation. On 29 November the Queen duly drove through London to St Paul's in state, with many thousands cheering her, although the Cathedral itself was half empty. She was permitted to sit on the bishop's throne, but the canon-in-residence declined to insert any special intention in the General Thanksgiving and she was not mentioned once during the service. When she left the Cathedral the organist played a series of variations on 'God Save the King' as the voluntary.

The King was considerably vexed with Liverpool at the dropping of the Bill. On 16 November he drafted, but did not despatch, a letter informing Lord Liverpool that he was seeking an alternative Government. The King seriously considered the possibility of inviting the Whigs to take office, and there remain, among his papers, two memoranda in which he lists the 'advantages' and 'the attendant evils' of a change of Government. The Whigs, he thought, would 'get rid of the question of the Queen speedily' and lessen 'the difficulties' of 'our domestic policy'; but they might urge him to free Napoleon from St Helena, to disavow the treaties and foreign alliances of the past five years, and to emancipate the Roman Catholics contrary to his own conscience and to the 'pure and exalted spirit of my revered father'. Moreover, he could not ignore the slights and ridicule to which many of the Whigs had subjected him: better Liverpool and Castlereagh in office than Grey and Brougham. By Christmas he had come to accept defeat and authorised the Government to put a royal residence at the Queen's disposal and settle the problem of her annuity; but he treated the Tory Ministers ungraciously for several months and ostentatiously welcomed the more moderate leaders of the Opposition to his private receptions.

For nine weeks after the Thanksgiving Service at St Paul's the King kept clear of the London streets. On 6 February 1821, he went to Drury Lane and was loudly applauded for several minutes; and two nights later he attended a play at Covent Garden. Mrs Arbuthnot, the Duke of Wellington's friend, was present in one of the boxes of the theatre and wrote in her journal, 'Nothing could be more beautiful than the appearance of the house crowded almost to suffocation, and the whole standing up and waving their hats and handkerchiefs for near a quarter of an hour.' It is true that someone in the Gallery called out 'Where's your wife, Georgie?' and that, on both nights, he thought it advisable for his carriage to be escorted by a troop of Life Guards; but, in general, it seemed as if the Caroline hysteria had died down; and the King decided that the coronation, which for obvious reasons had been postponed in the previous August, might now take place on 19 July 1821.

He applied all his gifts of showmanship to planning the coronation. It was the only pageant in his life in which he was the central figure, 'Sun King' for a day, and every detail followed his own fancy. The result, inevitably, was as confused as the architecture of the Pavilion: the ceremony owed something to Stuart precedents and much to Ivanhoe and Kenilworth. (It is fitting that Sir Walter Scott should have made the journey south for the occasion.) Parliament, rather surprisingly, granted nearly a quarter of a million pounds for the coronation service and festivities; and the King's only real worry was that the Queen might make a scene. Early in May she had written to Lord Liverpool to ask what 'ladies of high rank' would carry her train and 'what dress His Majesty would desire her to wear'; and she had taken the King's refusal to accord her any place in the ceremony extremely badly. On coronation day she drove to the Abbey and tried to gain admittance at each of the doors, but she was turned away because she had no ticket. Her demonstration provoked hostility from the crowd who, whatever they may have felt a few months earlier, now sensed that she had no place in the cast-list of this particular production and hooted her from the stage.

Apart from this tiresome interruption, all went well for the King. He had spent the night at the Speaker's House so as to be close to the Abbey. At 10.25 in the morning a procession set out from Westminster Hall for the service. It moved along a covered walk, raised three feet high, so that spectators might see kingship in all its splendour. The procession was headed by the Royal Herbwoman who, with six attendant maids, scattered nosegays along the route. They were followed by a Household Band and by the Corporation of the City of London (whose sympathies had so recently been elsewhere). Peers in full robes came next, with Privy Councillors who were not in the Lords following in a special costume of Elizabethan inspiration and royal design – the Foreign Secretary, Castlereagh, looked 'handsomer than ever' in white and blue satin with trunk hose. Dignitaries of State carried crown, orb, sceptre and sword: dignitaries of Church a patten, a chalice and a Bible. And then, at last came the King, walking slowly beneath a canopy of cloth-of-gold, his train of crimson velvet twenty-seven feet long relieved with a pattern of golden stars. His hat, 'vast and plumed and Spain-like', was decorated with ostrich feathers and his wig was so long and curled that it hung as a lion's mane over his bowed shoulders. Some of the younger generation, who had come 'inclined to giggle' at a fancy-dress parade, were 'affected in a manner they never dreamt of'; and the painter Benjamin Haydon was so captivated by the scene that he described his sovereign as 'like some gorgeous bird of the East'.

The ceremony in the Abbey lasted for five hours. The Archbishop of York, Dr Harcourt, preached a thunderous sermon on the need for the good ruler to preserve his subjects' morals 'from the contagion of vice and irreligion'. Unfortunately, from time to time the King's attention seems to have lapsed and two observers noticed him 'nodding and winking . . . and sighing and making eyes' at Lady Conyngham, whom almost everybody at Court seems to have detested. But he recovered his dignity during the final anthems and returned to Westminster Hall,

32 George 'Beau' Brummell, the Prince's friend and arbiter of taste. Brummell was responsible for introducing stiffening into cravats – 'When he first appeared in this stiffened cravat, its sensation was prodigious; dandies were struck dumb with envy, and washerwomen miscarried.' (*The English Spy*, 1826).

33 Charles James Fox, one of the Prince's closest friends. This portrait was painted by Hickel before 1798.

Despite his lack of success in the political arena, George always remained an important patron of the arts. He did much to encourage the Royal Academy, and built up his own collection of paintings. In particular, he purchased many examples of the seventeenth-century Dutch School. 34 (*left*) Detail of the chain of office presented by George to the Presidents of the Royal Academy. 35 (*below*) The Prince of Wales is escorted by Sir Joshua Reynolds, the President of the Royal Academy.

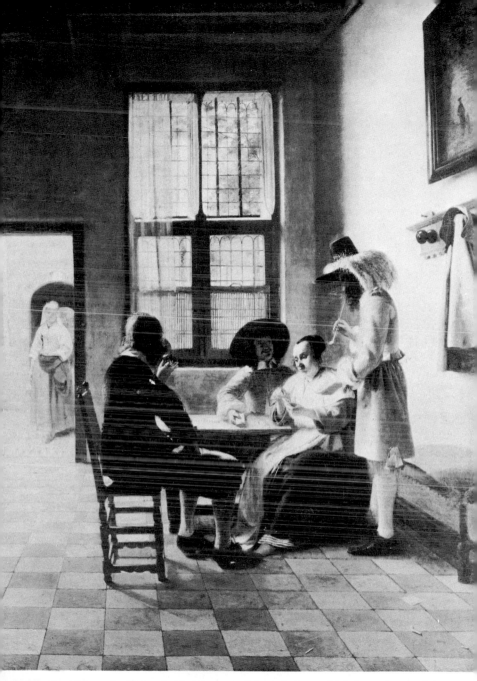

36 *The Card Players* by Pieter de Hooch, one of the paintings which formed part of the Prince's collection.

Two of the Prince's chief guests during the State visit of 1814. 37 (*left*) Prince Metternich, the Austrian minister, from a portrait by Sir Thomas Lawrence. 38 (*below*) Frederick William of Prussia, also by Sir Thomas Lawrence.

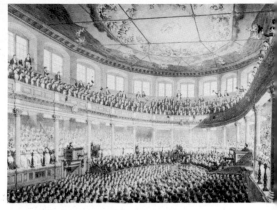

The English public looked upon Tsar Alexander I as the personification of Russia's defiance of Napoleon. His every move was fully recorded by the English press. 39 (*left*) Lawrence's portrait of Alexander I. 40 (*above*) The Tsar and the King of Prussia receiving degrees at the Sheldonian Theatre, Oxford, on 14 June 1814. 41 (*below*) The Tsar with his sister, the Grand Duchess Catherine, on the balcony of Pulteney's Hotel in Piccadilly.

42 (*above*) The first gas lighting appeared in Pall Mall in 1807, when Winsor's gas lamps were introduced.

43 (*below*) The Regent Street Quadrant, conceived by John Nash as part of his great scheme for a 'Royal Mile' stretching from Portland Place to Carlton House.

44 Portrait of John Nash by Sir Thomas Lawrence.

45 (*above*) Humphrey Repton's design for the Pavilion at Brighton. He took his ideas from Sezincote, a country house built in Hindu style by a retired member of the East India Company. Nash used Repton's designs as the basis for his reconstruction of the Pavilion.

47 (*above*) Watercolour showing the entrance to the Chain Pier at Brighton.

46 (*below*) Cross-section showing Nash's additions to the Pavilion.

48 (*above*) Cartoon alluding to Charlotte's marriage. The Prince Regent is pushing forward the reluctant Prince Leopold of Saxe-Coburg, while the Queen tries to encourage the Princess.

49 (*below*) Charlotte was married to Prince Leopold on 2 May 1816. This illustration shows the young couple at Covent Garden.

50 (*above*) Charlotte died in child-bed on 6 November 1817. The Prince Regent was so overcome by grief that he was unable to attend the funeral. The funeral procession from a contemporary painting.

51 (*below*) After Charlotte's death the question of the succession assumed great importance. The Regent's three unmarried brothers – the Dukes of Clarence, Cambridge and Kent – now made haste to take wives. Cruikshank has celebrated this in this savage satire, 'The Homburg Waltz', as their sister Princess Elizabeth had already set the fashion by marrying the Prince of Hesse-Homburg.

52 (*above left*) Queen Charlotte, a portrait by **Sir** Thomas Lawrence. Her death in November 1818 was a great blow to the Prince Regent, who missed her support.

53 (*above right*) Portrait of George III as an old man, living out his days alone in Windsor Castle.

54 (*below*) The coronation procession of George IV, wending its way from the Abbey to Westminster Hall. The King can be seen walking beneath a canopy of cloth-of-gold.

55 (*above*) Cartoon showing the King's desperate attempts to get himself divorced from Caroline, while Justice, blindfold, gives encouragement to the Queen.

56 (*below*) Sympathy for Caroline began to cool rapidly as the coronation day approached. When she sought entry into the Abbey she provoked hostility from the crowd. This *volte-face* can be detected in the cartoons – this savage cartoon shows Caroline with Pergami and Brougham in a most unsympathetic light.

57 (*left*) Sir Walter Scott, who master-minded the royal visit to Scotland. Portrait by Landseer, 1824.
58 (*below*) George IV set off for his State visit to Scotland in August 1822. This engraving by Havell shows his embarkation at Greenwich with the Royal Naval College in the left-hand background.

59 (*opposite above*) Towards the end of his life, George ceased to live at his Pavilion at Brighton and spent much more time at the Royal Lodge at Windsor, which he referred to as his cottage. He is shown in this cartoon welcoming his mistress, Lady Conyngham, to his 'lonely cot'.

In 1824, George decided to have Windsor Castle modernised and commissioned Sir Jeffry Wyatville to undertake the reconstruction. The Baroque apartments, laid out in Charles II's reign by Hugh May, were almost entirely swept away and replaced by rooms more to the King's taste.
60 (*opposite below*) The King's Audience Chamber at Windsor, as re-modelled by Wyatville

61 Princess Victoria, George IV's niece, god-daughter and eventual heir to the throne. George resented her at first, but overcame his hostility to her upon the death of her father, when she was only a few months old.

where three hundred and twelve male guests sat down to a massive banquet watched by the peeresses in the gallery (who must have been extremely hungry). Diners and spectators were entertained by the arrival of the Lord High Constable (Wellington), the Lord High Steward and the Deputy Earl Marshal on horseback and by the King's Champion on a white charger. The Champion threw down his gauntlet three times but very sensibly nobody took it up. The solemnity of the occasion was marred by the Deputy Earl Marshal's horse, which was affected in a manner many might have expected. Yet the whole ceremony was a remarkable triumph for the King's sense of majesty; and as his carriage carried him back, exhausted, to Carlton House there were wild scenes of enthusiasm. It is a little difficult to see what the mass of his subjects gained by the coronation festivities: but it was a warm night, there were fireworks in Hyde Park, and it had been a colourful and noisy day for them to remember.

The King, of course, enjoyed displaying himself on ceremonial occasions and he had already made it clear that he wished to travel during his reign rather than stay in the southern counties of England for year after year as his father had been content to do. He planned State Visits to Ireland (where none of his predecessors had landed except to wage war or impose pacification), to Scotland (where no reigning monarch had been since Stuart times) and to Hanover (unvisited by its ruler since 1758). He also considered making a courtesy call on the Austrian Emperor in Vienna and was tempted to accept Metternich's invitation to attend one of the Congresses which were a feature of Europe's diplomatic system in the post-war decade. Castlereagh, and several other members of the Cabinet, had no wish for the monarch to recover any initiative in foreign affairs and they discouraged all contacts between the King and the great autocratic dynasties of Europe. They remained suspicious of the King's interest in Continental politics and distrusted his close friendship with the Austrian ambassador, Prince Esterhazy, and with the Russian ambassador and his highly intelligent wife, Count and Countess Lieven. His Ministers, however, could hardly prevent the King of Hanover from setting foot in his own dominions, and they had the good sense to realise that royal journeys to Dublin and Edinburgh would have considerable political value at a time of such widespread unrest. The first State Visit would be to Ireland, which for the King meant the City of Dublin and Shane Castle, the Conyngham family seat twenty miles to the north.

On 31 July, only twelve days after the Coronation, the King accordingly embarked at Portsmouth in the *Royal George*, a yacht of some 300 tons displacement built for him at Deptford in 1817; and in the first week of August the vessel sailed slowly down the Channel, rounded Land's End and headed northwards for the Welsh coast. By 6 August the *Royal George* had reached Anglesey and anchored off Holyhead, preparatory to crossing the Irish Sea. Here, however, the King received unexpected news. On 30 July Queen Caroline was seized by abdominal pains, while attending a performance at Drury Lane. She was conveyed back to Brandenburg House, beside the Thames at Hammersmith, and by the end of the week it was clear she was dying. On learning of her illness, the King decided to remain in Anglesey until the situation became clearer; he did not wish to be denounced for having enjoyed a public celebration at such a time.

Queen Caroline died on the evening of 7 August. There were immediate difficulties over her funeral, for she had expressed a wish to be buried in Germany and to have engraved on her coffin the simple – but to the King 'offensive' – inscription 'Caroline of Brunswick, the injured Queen of England'. From Anglesey the King sensibly proposed that her body should be taken down river to the Nore on a state barge and embarked on a warship for the Elbe, thereby avoiding demonstrations in the streets. The Admiralty, however, had no suitable vessel available and the authorities decided to convey the Queen's body (in a coffin bearing the inscription she had chosen) to Harwich, where a ship was waiting; but they gave instructions that the funeral procession was to avoid central London and the City. The whole affair was hopelessly bungled. A mob of demonstrators forced the procession to turn down Tottenham Court Road and follow a route to Temple Bar, where the Lord Mayor 'paid honour to the Queen's remains'. During the disturbances and rioting, one man was killed. This sorry episode was in no way the fault of the King, who behaved with remarkable tact during the week of the funeral; but it afforded fresh material to his personal enemies, another callous tale for the black legend.

Meanwhile, on 12 August (his fifty-ninth birthday), the King crossed from Holyhead to Howth in a small packet-boat, for adverse winds kept the *Royal George* in harbour. Although the King made an excellent impromptu speech to the enthusiastic crowd that greeted him in Howth, he was careful to remain out of the public eye for five days of mourning before making a ceremonial entry into Dublin, dressed in the uniform he had designed for himself as a field-marshal, with a thick black armband and a massive spray of shamrock in his hat. The visit, which lasted until 3 September, was a considerable success. The Irish enjoyed all the showmanship of State and the King was delighted with everything he saw. Only the crossing back to the Pembrokeshire coast spoilt his pleasure, for the *Royal George* was caught in a heavy sea and the King (in his own words) was 'torn to pieces by the effects and sickness of an eight and forty hours tempest'. Surprisingly, he then decided that he would prefer to remain aboard and sail back to Portsmouth rather than be shaken in a carriage over Welsh roads. This was a great mistake as the tiny vessel was tossed around like a cork in a gale off Land's End and for a few hours the Duke of York, without knowing it, was very near succeeding to the throne. Eventually the King arrived at Carlton House on 16 September, thirteen days after leaving Dublin. He set out again for Hanover on 24 September, crossing from Ramsgate to Calais in the *Royal George*, with only a slight swell to recall recent discomforts.

His one and only Continental visit lasted for seven weeks. It began with a night at Dessin's Hotel in Calais (taking care to avoid the discredited Brummell) and continued with a short stay in Brussels, which enabled the King to make a detailed inspection of the field of Waterloo, with Wellington to guide him and torrential rain reminding the Duke of the eve of battle. Then on to Dusseldorf a Prussian garrison town set pleasantly amid open country, and north-eastwards into the Hanoverian territories, where communications were so poor that the horses had to be changed every five miles. At last, on 7 October, a hundred-and-one-gun salute welcomed the King of Hanover to his capital. He remained in residence until 28 October.

The King threw himself with heavy earnestness into everything Hanoverian: hunting was undertaken in a grand manner; good German tears were shed at the noble sentiments in a university address of welcome; and the prerogative of mercy was seen to be exercised to pardon minor criminals. But he was soon very, very bored. He was deeply touched by the loyalty of his German subjects: it was their solemn and conventional way of life which he found tedious. For the final week of his visit, however, he had more congenial company. Castlereagh – or, as he had now become, Lord Londonderry – had invited the Austrian Chancellor, Prince Metternich, to come to Hanover and discuss high politics; and George ɪv thoughtfully suggested that Countess Dorothea Lieven (whose husband was in Russia, reporting to the Tsar) might also travel to Hanover where her wit could entertain both the King, who had admired her for many years, and Metternich, whose mistress she had become during the Congress of Aix in 1818. There was accordingly a happy gathering, with the King flattering Metternich excessively and embracing him with more tenderness than he could ever remember; although both the Austrian Chancellor and Dorothea Lieven found it embarrassing to have to listen to sustained verbal onslaughts by the King of England upon all his Ministers except Londonderry. No important political decisions were taken. The King, however, so enjoyed the atmosphere of world politics that he told Metternich he had every intention of joining his brother sovereigns at the Congress to be held in northern Italy in the following autumn. But his enthusiasm for foreign travel was lessened by an agonising attack of gout, which made the homeward journey as unpleasant as the crossing from Dublin, though less dangerous. To embark on a series of stately progressions in one's sixtieth year imposes a severe physical strain; and the King remained at Brighton for most of the winter and much of the spring, convalescent and often irascible.

Yet, until the middle of June 1822, he had every intention of going to Vienna, and probably to Florence or Verona for the Congress as well. The Government, however, in difficulties with its former Russian and Austrian allies, was equally determined that he should not identify his person with Metternich's system; and Sir Walter Scott was encouraged to urge the King to visit Edinburgh that summer rather than cross to the Continent again. After several scenes of tears and tantrums, the King agreed in early July that he would sail up the east coast to the Firth of Forth. Poor Scott was given precisely a month in which to stir his unenthusiastic compatriots into welcoming the head of the House of Hanover by a living pageant of romantic history.

Sir Walter did well. He was an impresario as gifted as his sovereign; and the King enjoyed every moment of his fifteen days in Scotland. Although he stayed at Dalkeith Palace, outside Edinburgh, he used Holyroodhouse for State ceremonies and delighted his hosts by a splendid appearance on the battlements of Edinburgh Castle where, in pouring rain, he vigorously waved his field-marshal's hat to thousands cheering him in the outer courts below. At the levée in Holyroodhouse the King appeared in full Highland uniform and wearing Stuart tartan, with flesh-coloured tights ('pantaloons') under his kilt as a compromise between local practice and the decencies of royal decorum. He was genuine in his enthusiasm. For many years he had thrilled to the sound of bagpipes and admired Scottish reels; and, when he accepted an invitation to attend the Caledonian Hunt Ball, it was reported in the press that he had insisted, 'No foreign dances. I dislike seeing anything in Scotland that is not purely national and characteristic.'

It was easy – and is easier still today – to mock the self-conscious 'Scott-ishness' of the visit: the command performance of Rob Roy; the Highland chiefs lodged by Sir Walter at Abbotsford to give an authentic Gaelic touch; the antiquarian diligence which revived forgotten ceremonials at a time when steamboats were beginning to ply between Leith and London. But the combined tact of Sir Walter and the King had two important consequences: like the Dublin visit of 1821, it gave the lie to the caricature of George iv as a selfish Falstaff; and it completed the reconciliation between the monarch and his Scottish subjects. When the Royal George landed the King at Greenwich on 2 September he carried with him a knife and fork and spoon used by the Young Pretender in 1745. These were strange relics for the godson of Butcher Cumberland to cherish.

8

Royal Lodge 1822–30

The King returned from Scotland in the autumn of 1822 to a major crisis in the Government. On 12 August – George IV's birthday – Lord Londonderry (Castlereagh) committed suicide by cutting his throat with a penknife. For ten years he had carried the burden of foreign affairs as well as acting as Leader of the House of Commons (for he was an Irish peer, never a member of the House of Lords). The strain of a long Parliamentary session and of important diplomatic exchanges over the problems of Turkey and Spain tired a sensitive and conscientious mind; and in the previous week both the King and the Duke of Wellington had noted his wild conversation and strange behaviour. To many of his countrymen Castlereagh was a personification of political reaction, and small groups of radical demonstrators even cheered as his coffin was brought into Westminster Abbey on the day of his funeral. But to the King his suicide was a bitter blow. He was well aware of the respect which Castlereagh's finely balanced judgment had won among the leading European statesmen; and he was only too conscious that, more than anybody else, Castlereagh had served as a mediator between the Crown and Lord Liverpool's Government at times when their relations with each other were far from friendly. It was difficult to find a successor either at the Foreign Office or as Leader of the Commons; and the King was anxious that nothing should be settled in a hurry.

He may well have hoped that Castlereagh's tragic death would precipitate the fall of the Government. Had that been so, he would almost certainly have invited Wellington to form a coalition ministry, for he tended in these early years of his reign to look upon the Duke as the one trustworthy spokesman in either party. As it was, the King had to be content with pressing Wellington's claims to the Foreign Office rather than to the premiership, a post which Liverpool had no intention of surrendering so long as his health held out. Liverpool, indeed, was not inclined to accommodate the King's wishes over reconstruction of the Government. To the King's subsequent annoyance, he began discussions before the *Royal George* arrived back from Scotland and he showed a sound civilian suspicion of the military hero's ambitions in politics. Wellington might be entrusted with important diplomatic missions to Vienna, Verona and St Petersburg and he could continue to hold Cabinet rank as 'Master-General of the Ordnance'; but Liverpool had no doubt that Castlereagh's successor at the Foreign Office should be George Canning. It was, unfortunately, a name almost anathema to the King.

Canning had spent nearly thirty years in the House of Commons, originally as a Pittite Tory of liberal inclination. He had been Foreign Secretary from 1807 to 1809 and had never incurred the unpopularity of his more conservative-minded colleagues. He possessed a felicitous turn of phrase and a lively independence of mind and spirit. But he had long been regarded with distrust by the King. Canning had befriended Caroline in her early days at Blackheath and she had consented to be godmother to his eldest son. Nor had his attitude towards her changed in later years. Although holding minor office in the Government he had absented himself from the country during the 'Queen's Trial' and had then resigned in December 1820 because he did not think the Government was making a sufficiently generous response to the Queen's claims after the withdrawal of the Bill of Pains and Penalties. His personal friends included City dignitaries in London who had formerly been among Caroline's most ostentatious champions. There was, indeed, much in Canning's background which the King found hard to forget. But, whatever his personal feelings might be, George IV took his responsibilities as a constitutional monarch seriously, and when he saw that Liverpool felt a need to have Canning at the Foreign Office he withdrew his objections, though hardly gracefully. 'Mr Canning's readmission into the Cabinet' entailed 'the greatest personal sacrifice that a sovereign ever made to a subject, or indeed, taking all *the circumstances*, that man ever made to man', the King wrote to his Lord Chancellor on 9 September with characteristic hyperbole. Canning might be at the Foreign Office, but for three years a contest was to continue between sovereign and minister before they began to understand each other.

Canning's appointment accelerated a diplomatic revolution. His predecessor had collaborated, when possible, with the Eastern autocracies (Austria, Prussia and Russia) in their attempts to maintain an orderly system of repressive government throughout the Continent. But Canning wished to make a dramatic break in this policy. 'For "Europe",' he declared, 'I shall be desirous now and again to read "England".' This was a sentiment which most of his compatriots would have applauded; but the King genuinely thought that much of Canning's policy was disastrous. It seemed to ignore the link between George IV's British and Hanoverian territories. Quite apart from pride and sentiment, isolation was a luxury which the King literally could not afford: he was able, on his Hanoverian assets, to raise a considerable loan from the banking-house of Rothschild in November 1823. He found himself opposing Canning on grounds of self-interest and political conviction as much as of personal antipathy.

At first Canning made some attempt to placate his sovereign: he offered a vacant Under-Secretaryship of State to the son of Lady Conyngham. The post was accepted but the gesture was a little too crude for the King. In January 1823 he told Countess Lieven (or so she reported to Metternich) that Canning was 'a clever man . . . trying to win me over' but he added: 'He is plebeian and has no manners; as for his brilliant repartees, I have never heard any. He dined here and said nothing but yes and no.' Two months later the King was complaining again to the Countess: 'I do not like him better than I did. I recognise his talents, and I believe we need him in the Commons; but he is no more capable of conducting foreign affairs than your baby.' And in the summer the King went out of his way to scorn and humiliate Canning in the presence of foreign ambassadors at a ball at Carlton House.

A year later their relations were no better. There was an angry explosion over the civilities to be shown to two unusual visitors to Europe in June 1824 when, according to Wellington, the King abused Canning behind his back, saying 'Think of that damned fellow wanting me to have the King and Queen of the Sandwich Islands to dinner, as if I would sit at table with such a pair of damned cannibals.' More serious conflicts followed, with the King deliberately encouraging opposition in the Cabinet to Canning's attempts to support, by diplomatic means, the struggle for independence of the ex-Spanish colonies in Latin America. By the winter of 1824–5 Canning had come to recognise that most of his efforts were being hampered by the intrigues of what he called 'the Cottage Clique', the King's most frequent guests at the Royal Lodge, Windsor, where George IV tended to spend far more time than in earlier years. Constitutionally this was a dangerous development, reminiscent of the later Stuarts rather than of the faction-jostling manœuvres of the first three Georges.

Apart from the King himself, there were some eight or nine members of the 'Cottage Clique': the Russian ambassador and his wife, Count and Countess Lieven; the Hanoverian Minister, Count Munster; the Austrian ambassador, Paul Esterhazy, and his wife (who was a distant cousin of the King); the French ambassador (Polignac); the King's current favourite, Lady Conyngham; and the Duke of Wellington. To these personal friends of the sovereign it might be correct to add Sir William Knighton, the King's physician and, as Keeper of the Privy Purse, his unofficial secretary; but Knighton's intelligence held him back from the more intemperate intrigues of the group and, to some extent, he had succeeded Castlereagh as the Government's go-between at Court. The creation of the Cottage Clique was a rash political move on the King's part and may even have been accidental. He always maintained that his constitutional functions as King of Hanover were distinct from his obligations as ruler of the United Kingdom. As Hanover's Prince, he believed himself entitled to correspond directly with the rulers of Austria, Russia and France through their representatives accredited to him in London and without informing the British Government of what he said or did. Had the King confined himself to Germanic affairs in this correspondence, it would be difficult to find fault with his reasoning; but he made it clear to foreign rulers that he could not approve of Canning's attitude towards the Eastern Question or the sympathy which he was showing, in the name of His Majesty's Government, for liberal constitutionalism in Spain and Portugal. The King used his contacts to plot against Canning personally and against his policy; and rumours of the Cottage Clique's activity began to appear in the London Press as early as April 1823. The frequent presence of the Duke of Wellington at the Royal Lodge is particularly hard to justify, for the Duke was still a member of Liverpool's Cabinet and therefore a colleague of Canning, against whom he was intriguing.

Tension between the King and Canning reached a climax at the end of January 1825 when the Foreign Secretary urged the Government to recognise the independence of the ex-Spanish Colonies. The King sent a stormy letter to Liverpool wishing 'to know from his Cabinet, individually, whether the great principles of policy established by his Government in the years 1814, 1815 and 1818 *are, or are not, to be abandoned*'. Canning, at the next Cabinet meeting, complained that a clique of foreigners was seeking to force him from office and threatened to go down to the House of Commons 'with the letter in his pocket and move an address to the King to know who had advised him to write the letter'. Wellington, disturbed by Canning's belligerency, advised the King to give way and accept the recognition of independence in Latin America; and the King, having sent a formal message of displeasure for Liverpool to convey to Canning, dutifully did as Wellington wished. He had suffered yet another political defeat at the hands of Liverpool and his Ministers; and he was more determined than ever before to keep on good terms with Wellington, the Prime Minister of the future. Meanwhile, Sir William Knighton advised the King to seek a reconciliation with Canning, whose words and actions were rapidly making him the most popular Minister for more than twenty years.

But in the early spring of 1825 the King made one last attempt to discredit Canning and provoke him into resignation. With the active support of Dorothea Lieven and of Wellington, the King invited Metternich (who was in Paris at the time) to cross from Dieppe to Brighton and travel directly to the Royal Lodge at Windsor, where the King of Hanover could talk to him about the affairs of Europe without involving his British Foreign Minister, twenty miles away at Westminster. This absurd scheme, which owed much to the mischievous meddling of Countess Lieven, was politically dangerous and would have produced an outburst of xenophobic indignation in the London Press had it been revealed. Canning, suspecting what was planned, sent an indirect warning to Metternich through the British ambassador in Paris: 'I wonder whether he [Metternich] is aware that the private communication of foreign Ministers with the King of England is wholly at variance with the spirit, and practice too, of the British Constitution.' Metternich took the hint and stayed away. It was left to Sir William Knighton to seek to extricate his royal master from another embarrassing defeat; and, at the end of April, Knighton visited Canning (who was unwell and in bed at the time) so as to assure him of the King's confidence in his Minister's judgment. The plots which had so annoyed Canning were part of a clumsy conspiracy engineered by Metternich – or so he was given to understand.

Canning was too good a politician to reject Knighton's olive branch. He needed George IV's support, if possible, against the ultra-Tories in the Cabinet; and the King had begun to see that if he openly approved of Canning's policy then some of the popularity of the Minister would be reflected on the Crown. By the autumn George IV had begun to admit that Canning had raised his royal prestige by pursuing a policy of greater independence than Castlereagh. And by the summer of 1826 Canning was completely in the King's favour: he was even invited to spend a couple of days at the Royal Lodge, together with his younger son (who was still at Eton) and his son-in-law, a notorious gambler with a dubious reputation. Once he had accepted Canning, the King delighted in his wit. As Leader of the Commons, Canning had to keep his sovereign informed of its proceedings, a task which poor Castlereagh had performed with painstaking boredom. Canning, however, made the Parliamentary reports a source of entertainment and the King enjoyed reading them, much as his niece was to enjoy Disraeli's notes from Downing Street half a century later. The two men found they understood each other well, even though the King retained mental reservations over his Minister's reformist principles. It was convenient to have a Foreign Secretary who immediately perceived the advantage of appointing a tiresome admirer of Lady Conyngham to a vacant diplomatic post in Buenos Aires. By the end of 1826 it was clear that Canning, with his reputation in Parliament and his ascendancy over the King, was the most likely successor to Liverpool and that Wellington had fallen from favour; but it was a pity that for the past fourteen years Canning had made no secret of his sympathy for Catholic Emancipation; for the King still insisted that his conscience and his respect for his father's memory would not permit him to remove Roman Catholic disabilities.

It would, of course, be a mistake to think of George IV as interested solely in the cut and thrust of political intrigues during these years. He still saw himself as a noble patron of literature and the arts. In January 1823 he presented to the nation the splendid library of nearly seventy thousand volumes which George III had collected over half a century.

It was left to the Government to find a suitable building in which to house the books. Since 1759 the exhibits of a British Museum had been collected in Montague House, Bloomsbury, and it was now decided to replace Montague House by constructing a dignified series of galleries and libraries, worthy of a great national collection. Work on the King's Library of the British Museum accordingly began late in 1823, but the famous southern colonnade was not finished until seventeen years after George IV's death. The King was also indirectly responsible for encouraging the foundation of the National Gallery, for in 1823 he cajoled the Liverpool Government into buying the paintings collected by Sir Julius Angerstein, and these form the nucleus of the Gallery's display. For many years the King had urged successive ministers to establish a permanent art exhibition in the capital but the building of the National Gallery itself did not start until 1832. George IV had, however, some right to be considered a founding father of the Collection and it is appropriate that the colonnade which formerly stood outside Carlton House should still today form the principal entrance to the Gallery.

The King's artistic tastes mellowed with the passing of the years; and the slightly vulgar ostentation of the later Regency gave way to a timeless and impersonal dignity. In 1822 the Royal Pavilion at Brighton was at last finished; and yet, almost immediately, the King seemed to lose his affection for the place. There appear to have been several reasons for his change of mood: the growth of the town destroyed the Pavilion's privacy; Lady Conyngham was never at ease in Brighton, where she imagined herself insulted; and the King seems to have thought that the exposed position of the Pavilion was a temptation to any would-be assassin, especially in the summer months. He continued to pay short visits, and we still read of happy and domesticated evenings in the letters and diaries of Society figures; but now it was a case of musical parties (to meet Signor Rossini, for example) rather than the long banquets of earlier years. On 7 March 1827 George IV left the Pavilion for Windsor; and 'the Kremlin by the sea' remained unoccupied until his brother's accession in 1830.

Nor was Brighton alone neglected. George IV gradually tired of Carlton House, particularly after it was damaged by fire in 1825. Although he thought it an admirable residence for the heir to the throne, it was too small for royal grandeur. He decided to pull down Carlton House stone by stone, erect a terrace of elegant private houses on the site, and trust that their rent would provide compensation to the Crown for some of the fortune lavished on Carlton House in the past. Meanwhile after considering the merits of a new State Residence in Green Park, he commissioned John Nash to convert Buckingham House into a palace. Unfortunately both the architect and his royal patron were too old to give Buckingham Palace the attention which they had lavished on earlier projects; and the design was still unfinished when the King died.

Throughout most of his reign George IV's principal architectural interests were concentrated around Windsor. During the early years the Cottage (Royal Lodge) was transformed into a comfortable home, with Cumberland Lodge as an annexe a third of a mile away, and with long avenues laid out across the Great Park to Virginia Water. Here the King, driving his own pony phaeton or sitting back in a landau, could enjoy a sense of spaciousness denied him at Brighton. There was little risk in Windsor Park of some prying eyes mocking the gross figure pathetically pursuing harmless pleasures, talking to Lady Conyngham about Ascot and horses, or his designs for new tunics for the Guards, or the latest historical novel by the indefatigable Sir Walter. The Royal Lodge was to George IV what the Trianon had been to the Bourbons in the previous century; but he needed a Versailles close at hand for State occasions and, in 1824, he accordingly resolved to have Windsor Castle modernised, sweeping away the last traces of the medieval fortress where his father had lived and died. Between 1824 and 1828 Sir Jeffry Wyatville changed the whole character of the Castle: the Round Tower was raised by some thirty feet; a series of State Apartments replaced the small drawing-rooms and dark music-rooms which were full of so many hollow memories; and the Waterloo Chamber was built as a final tribute to Victory, a fitting home for the portraits of Allied sovereigns, statesmen and soldiers which the Prince Regent had commissioned from Sir Thomas Lawrence as soon as the wars were over. By 1828 the King was able to reside in state at the Castle. The fact that he still preferred to live in the Royal Lodge is no reflection on the work of Wyatville.

From the King's letters and the memoirs of the period it does not seem as if he was often happy, let alone spiritually at ease. He knew that Lady Conyngham was an opportunist with little real affection for him: he tolerated her presence because he was accustomed to it and far too indolent by now to face changes in habit; and possibly he gained some consolation from the pious religiosity of her trivial mind. He found greater intellectual satisfaction in the barbed tongue of Dorothea Lieven and the company of Emily Cowper, who was a daughter of his old friend Lady Melbourne, and eventually wife to Lord Palmerston and supreme political hostess of London in the 'fifties. Sometimes the King's spirits were sufficiently roused for him to mimic Ministers past and present (long his principal social diversion) and occasionally he would play a hand at *écarté*, but he spent many hours reading and dozing in bed. From 1824 onwards he was frequently in pain, suffering both from gout and from troubles in the bladder. To relieve the discomfort he took larger and larger doses of laudanum, which inevitably made him drowsier still and it was not unknown for Ministers to undertake the journey from London to Windsor at his request only to find their sovereign too weary to give them an audience. The King, with his face a mask of rouge and grease-paint, became increasingly sensitive to the gaze of his subjects. It is possible that one of the reasons why he cut himself off from old friends – and, in particular, from Maria Fitzherbert – was self-conscious sorrow at his own appearance. From the autumn of 1828 onwards his eyesight began to fail, as his father's had done; and some of the London newspapers did not hesitate to suggest that he was showing some of the mental instability of George III as well. There is, however, no reason for supposing that he suffered from delusions to any greater extent than in earlier years. Physically he was decaying rapidly by his sixty-fifth birthday, and there seemed little likelihood that he would complete the biblical three score years and ten.

Yet there is much in the King's personality which remains puzzling. Until the summer of 1829 he continued to give an annual Juvenile Ball in London, an occasion for which he would journey up from Royal Lodge in order to play the part of some affably remote universal uncle, much as he had done in Brighton twenty years previously. He was genuinely interested in the sons and daughters of his friends, although (as ever) inclined to expansive gestures of generosity. Probably, at heart, he grieved for Charlotte, and for his stillborn grandson. It may well be that consciousness of leaving no heir to the throne intensified his love of building, as if he were seeking a material monument of dignity which might compensate for the disappointments of his private life.

He was unsure of how to treat his niece and god-daughter, Victoria. At her baptism, in June 1819, he had shown resentment at the proposal that she might be given the names 'Georgiana Charlotte Augusta Alexandrina Victoria' because he had no wish to hear a version of his own name, nor any mention of his deceased daughter, on such an occasion. But he soon overcame his hostility towards 'little Drina', especially as her father (his younger brother, the Duke of Kent) died from pneumonia seven months after the christening.

Queen Victoria herself, writing forty-six years later, could remember Royal Lodge as it was in the last week of July 1826, observed with all the clarity of a child of seven:

> We went to Cumberland Lodge, the King living at the Royal Lodge . . . When we arrived at the Royal Lodge the King took me by the hand, saying 'Give me your little paw.' He was large and gouty but with a wonderful dignity and charm of manner. He wore the wig which was so much worn in those days. Then he said he would give me something for me to wear, and that was his picture set in diamonds, which were worn by the Princesses as an order to a blue ribbon on the left shoulder. I was very proud of this – and Lady Conyngham pinned it on my shoulder.

Later in the week Victoria went to Virginia Water from Cumberland Lodge and there she had another exciting day with 'Uncle King':

> Then we . . . met the King in his phaeton in which he was driving the Duchess of Gloucester – and he said 'Pop her in,' and I was lifted in and placed between him and Aunt Gloucester, who held me round the waist. (Mamma was much frightened.) I was greatly pleased . . . We drove round the nicest part of Virginia Water and stopped at the Fishing Temple. Here there was a large barge and everyone went on board and fished, while a band played in another!

The waspish Dorothea Lieven, writing to Metternich at the time of 'Drina's' visit, declared: 'In spite of the caresses the King lavished on her, I could see that he did not like dandling on his sixty-four-year-old knee this little bit of the future, aged seven'; but there is no evidence of any lack of affection between uncle and niece. The King was always concerned over the health of the young Princess, though he had little liking or sympathy for her mother.

The public saw little of George IV in the last three years of his life, but his days were neither peaceful nor contented. In February 1827 Lord Liverpool suffered a stroke, from which he only partially recovered, and on 28 March Lady Liverpool formally notified the King of her husband's wish to resign office. It had long been assumed that the King would turn naturally to Wellington as Liverpool's successor, especially since the alternative candidate (Canning) had never modified his support of Catholic Emancipation to curry royal favour. But George IV hesitated; he sensed that the public mood preferred the commoner to the Duke, the man of peace to the man of war. On 12 April, still undecided, the King took to his bed. He agreed, however, to receive Canning who rallied him with the splendid exhortation: 'Sir, your father broke the domination of the Whigs. I hope your Majesty will not endure that of the Tories.' He assured the King that although his views were unchanged on the Catholic Question, the matter would not be raised in the present session of Parliament; and on 1 May Canning took office at the head of a Cabinet containing eight 'conservatives' (as he described them) and four Whigs.

Given good health Canning might well have guided the King into accepting civil liberties for Catholics and a measure of Parliamentary reform; but the new Prime Minister was a sick man and could achieve little. On 8 August, after fourteen weeks of office, he died. The King thereupon invited Lord Goderich, once Liverpool's Chancellor of the Exchequer, to form a Government which he believed he could himself dominate from Windsor. It was a dismal failure. The only remarkable quality possessed by 'Goody' Goderich was an ability to weep more frequently and more copiously than his sovereign. After four lachrymose months of dispute within the Cabinet, Goderich offered, and hurriedly withdrew, his resignation. It was by then the second half of December and the King, very sensibly, declared that he could see no reason why he should be the only person in the kingdom not permitted to eat his Christmas dinner in peace. He accordingly refused to take Goderich's action seriously. But, within a fortnight, Goderich was back at Windsor with a fresh plea to be released from office. This time the King felt bound to accept his resignation – and thoughtfully lent Goderich a royal handkerchief with which to stem his tears.

There now seemed to the King no alternative to Wellington and the Tories. He sent for the Duke on 9 January 1828, and received him propped up in bed and wearing a grease-stained turban and a silk dressing-gown: 'Arthur,' he declared, 'the Cabinet is defunct'; and he invited him to form a Government which would leave the Catholic Question unresolved. After due consultation, the Duke accepted and at fifty-eight became the first and, as yet, only Field Marshal to serve as Prime Minister of the United Kingdom.

But Westminster required different qualities of leadership from Waterloo. Within two months the Duke and the King were exchanging strained notes on the Catholic Question and by the end of 1828 Wellington had come to believe that only Catholic relief could avert civil war in Ireland. The King was furious: emancipation ran counter to the views of 'my revered and sainted father' he explained to the Home Secretary, Robert Peel; and he claimed that he had a duty to veto any such measure. Early in March 1829 the King took the last political initiative of his reign. He summoned his chief ministers to Windsor. For six hours he lectured them, not always relevantly, on the need to uphold the Protestant faith. His technique of persuasion included tears, kisses, brandy, sips of water, threats of abdication, more brandy, pleas for divine assistance, and a reverie on the delights of retiring to Hanover. In the end he dismissed them all from office, and from the royal presence. A few hours later, realising 'the country would be left without an administration', he wrote to his 'dear Friend', Wellington, and agreed reluctantly to accept Catholic Emancipation, to which he gave formal statutory consent in April.

All this hysteria sapped his energy and he never really recovered his health. By the autumn of 1829 Knighton, who saw him more than any-one else, knew that the King's heart was flaccid; and that September he sent a significant message to the Theatre Royal, Covent Garden, not to bother with the proposed reconstruction of the Royal Box 'for this year at least'. In the following April the King began to suffer a series of minor strokes and everyone knew that his massive frame could not long survive the strain. At Windsor he received an affectionate letter from Maria Fitzherbert who travelled to London in case he wished to see her; but he would not face emotional interviews. He praised the good taste of the prayers which were being said for his health; and bravely awaited death. It came for him, at Windsor Castle, in the small hours of 26 June 1830.

'Poor Prinney is really dead – on a Saturday too,' recorded Creevey with an awesome sigh. And Sir Walter Scott wrote in his journal, 'The whole day of pleasure was damped by the news of the King's death.' Yet few people mourned his passing. He had meant more to the country as Prince Regent than as King; and it was to be nearly a century before the public began to appreciate the full heritage of his mania for building and the decorative arts. In death he remained an enigma even to those who had known him closely. Wellington told Minnie Seymour, with evident surprise, how he had noticed a miniature glittering on his sovereign's breast and found it to be a likeness of Maria Fitzherbert. It was buried with him in the vault at Windsor; and, in her house in Brighton, a grey-haired widow wept bitterly when she heard Wellington's story.

HOUSE OF HANOVER

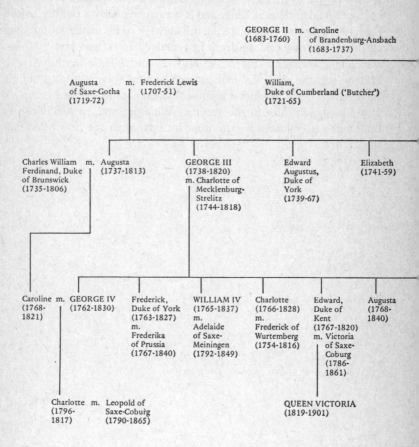

GEORGE II m. Caroline
(1683-1760)   of Brandenburg-Ansbach
(1683-1737)

Augusta   m. Frederick Lewis   William,
of Saxe-Gotha   (1707-51)   Duke of Cumberland ('Butcher')
(1719-72)   (1721-65)

Charles William   m. Augusta   GEORGE III   Edward   Elizabeth
Ferdinand, Duke   (1737-1813)   (1738-1820)   Augustus,   (1741-59)
of Brunswick   m. Charlotte of   Duke of
(1735-1806)   Mecklenburg-   York
                             Strelitz   (1739-67)
                             (1744-1818)

Caroline m. GEORGE IV   Frederick,   WILLIAM IV   Charlotte   Edward,   Augusta
(1768-   (1762-1830)   Duke of York   (1765-1837)   (1766-1828)   Duke of   (1768-
1821)   (1763-1827)   m.   m.   Kent   1840)
                        m.   Adelaide   Frederick of   (1767-1820)
                        Frederika   of Saxe-   Wurtemberg   m. Victoria
                        of Prussia   Meiningen   (1754-1816)   of Saxe-
                        (1767-1840)   (1792-1849)   Coburg
                                                    (1786-
                                                    1861)

Charlotte m. Leopold of   QUEEN VICTORIA
(1796-   Saxe-Coburg   (1819-1901)
1817)   (1790-1865)

5 daughters

William
Henry,
Duke of
Gloucester
(1743-1805)

Henry
Frederick,
Duke of
Cumberland
(1745-90)

Louisa
Anne
(1749-68)

Frederick
William
(1750-65)

Caroline
Matilda
(1751-75)

Elizabeth
(1770-
1840)
m.
Frederick
of Hesse-
Homburg
(1769-
1829)

Ernest,
Duke of
Cumberland
(1771-1851)
(King of
Hanover from
1837)

Augustus,
Duke of
Sussex
(1773-
1843)

Adolphus,
Duke of
Cambridge
(1774-1850)
m.
Augusta
of Hesse-
Cassel
(1797-1889)

Mary
(1776-
1857)
m.
William,
Duke of
Gloucester
(1776-
1834)

Sophia
(1777-
1848)

Octavius
(1779-
1843)

Alfred
(1780-82)

Amelia
(1783-
1810)

SELECT BIBLIOGRAPHY

PRIMARY SOURCES

Aspinall, A., *Correspondence of George, Prince of Wales* (Cassell, 1963–71)
    Letters of King George IV, 1812–30 (C.U.P., 1938)
    Letters of Princess Charlotte, 1811–17 (Home & Van Thal, 1949)
Bamford, F. and Wellington, Duke of, *The Journal of Mrs Arbuthnot, 1820–32* (Macmillan, 1950)
Gore, John, *Life and Times of Creevey* (Murray, 1937)
Harris, James, Earl of Malmesbury, *Diaries and Correspondence* (Bentley, 1844)
Knighton, Lady, *Memoirs of Sir William Knighton* (Bentley, 1838)
Lever, Sir T., *Correspondence of Lady Palmerston* (Murray, 1957)
Maxwell, Sir H., *The Creevy Papers* (Murray, 1903)
Papendieck, Charlotte, *Court and Private Life in the Time of Queen Charlotte* (Bentley, 1887)
Quennell, Peter, *Private Letters of Princess Lieven to Metternich* (Murray, 1937)
Strachey, L. and Fulford, R., *The Grenville Memoirs* (Macmillan, 1938)
Temperley, Harold, *Unpublished Diary of Princess Lieven* (Cape, 1935)

SECONDARY SOURCES

Chenevix Trench, Charles, *The Royal Malady* (Longmans, 1964)
Fulford, R., *George the Fourth* (Duckworth, revised edition 1949)
    The Trial of Queen Charlotte (Batsford, 1968)
Hobhouse, Christopher, *Fox* (Constable and Murray, 1947)
Plumb, J. H., *The First Four Georges* (Batsford, 1956)
Priestley, J. B., *The Prince of Pleasure* (Heinnemann, 1969)
Richardson, Joanna, *George IV, A Portrait* (Sidgwick & Jackson, 1966)

Roberts, Henry D., *The Royal Pavilion, Brighton* (Country Life, 1939)

Rolo, P. J. V., *George Canning* (Macmillan, 1965)

Sitwell, Sir O. and Barton, M., *Brighton* (Faber, 1935)

Summerson, John, *John Nash, Architect to King George IV* (Allen & Unwin, 1935)

Webster, Sir C., *The Foreign Policy of Castlereagh* (Bell, 1925–31)

INDEX